MANNED SPACEFLIGHT

AN EXPLORER'S GUIDE TO THE UNIVERSE

MANNED SPACEFLIGHT

EDITED BY ERIK GREGERSEN, ASSOCIATE EDITOR, ASTRONOMY AND SPACE EXPLORATION

Britannica®
Educational Publishing

IN ASSOCIATION WITH

ROSEN
EDUCATIONAL SERVICES

Published in 2010 by Britannica Educational Publishing
(a trademark of Encyclopædia Britannica, Inc.)
in association with Rosen Educational Services, LLC
29 East 21st Street, New York, NY 10010.

Distributed exclusively by Rosen Educational Services.
For a listing of additional Britannica Educational Publishing titles, call toll free (800) 237-9932.

First Edition

Britannica Educational Publishing
Michael I. Levy: Executive Editor
Marilyn L. Barton: Senior Coordinator, Production Control
Steven Bosco: Director, Editorial Technologies
Lisa S. Braucher: Senior Producer and Data Editor
Yvette Charboneau: Senior Copy Editor
Kathy Nakamura: Manager, Media Acquisition
Erik Gregersen: Associate Editor, Astronomy and Space Exploration

Rosen Educational Services
Jeanne Nagle: Senior Editor
Nelson Sá: Art Director
Matthew Cauli: Designer
Introduction by Corona Brezina

Library of Congress Cataloging-in-Publication Data

Manned spaceflight / edited by Erik Gregersen.—1st ed.
    p. cm.—(An explorer's guide to the universe)
Includes index.
"In association with Britannica Educational Publishing, Rosen Educational Services."
ISBN 978-1-61530-000-6 (library binding)
1. Astronautics—History—Juvenile literature. 2. Manned spaceflight—History—Juvenile literature. 3. Astronauts—Biography—Juvenile literature. I. Gregersen, Erik.
TL793.M265 2010
629.45—dc22

                                                            2009023566

On the cover: American astronaut Clay Anderson works on the International Space Station (ISS). Manned spaceflight has evolved from simple orbital expeditions to missions such as those that made construction of the ISS possible. *NASA*

CONTENTS

42

85

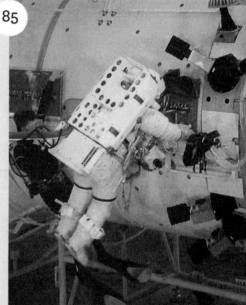

97

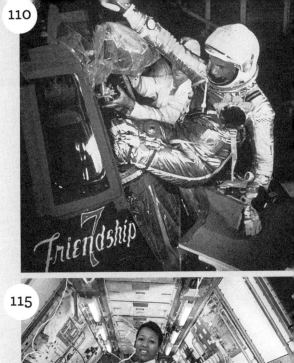

110

115

120

163

164

172

INTRODUCTION

The story of manned spaceflight is a tale of visionaries, scientists, and heroes. Marked by stunning triumphs and occasionally punctuated with tragedy, the saga created by exploring what lies beyond Earth's boundaries remains unrivaled by any fictional adventure. Within these pages, readers will discover an unfailingly detailed account of this glorious endeavour, from the first launch of unmanned spacecraft to the establishment of the International Space Station and beyond.

A few creative souls had tried to capture the thrill of space travel even before it had officially begun. Decades before the first manmade objects reached space, imaginative, and sometimes prophetic, writers and artists speculated about the future of space exploration. Books and magazine articles described scenarios in which humans would fly into space, establish space stations, and go on to colonize the Moon and other planets. People watched humans explore the Moon in the 1950 sci-fi movie *Destination Moon*. In 1968, one year before the lunar landing, the movie *2001: A Space Odyssey* envisioned a future in which humans could easily travel between Earth, a space station orbiting Earth, and a Moon base.

The expectations of ordinary Americans lagged behind these futuristic speculations. In 1949, a survey showed that less than half of the people polled believed that humans would reach the Moon by 2000. However, in 1957, an event occurred that galvanized efforts to develop an American space program. On October 4 of that year, the Soviets launched Sputnik, the first satellite to orbit Earth.

Sputnik was a 184-pound (83 kg) sphere that communicated to a ground station by shortwave radio. Americans were stunned by this demonstration of Soviet technological superiority. More than a beeping orb, Sputnik was a symbol of Soviet progress in the Cold War. The satellite's launch marked the beginning of the space race between the Soviet Union and the United States, the world's two superpowers.

At first, the Soviets maintained their lead. One month after launching Sputnik, they sent another satellite into space containing the first space traveler—a small dog named Laika. The Soviets were able to monitor Laika's respiration, heart rate, and other life signs, and they reported that she survived the conditions of space. One month later, on December 6, the United States Navy attempted to put its first test satellite into space using a rocket called

The space shuttle Atlantis *continues the tradition of manned space missions begun decades before.* istockphoto.com

the Vanguard. During the launch, the Vanguard rocket began to rise off of the pad, then it toppled over and exploded.

The Soviets again beat the Americans into space in 1961, sending Yury Gagarin into orbit before safely landing back on Earth. Meanwhile, the the National Aeronautics and Space Administration (NASA) was also working on putting astronauts into space via Project Mercury, created in 1958. Three weeks after Gagarin's flight, Alan Shepard became the first American in space, reentering Earth's atmosphere after 15 minutes. In 1962, John Glenn became the first American to orbit Earth.

These initial forays into space amazed people across the globe, but soon simply orbiting the planet was not enough. The United States and the Soviet Union shifted their focus to a long-range space enterprise: landing a man on the Moon.

During this period, both the American and Soviet space programs benefited from a firm commitment by their governments. Success in space was a matter of international prestige. In 1961, Pres. John F. Kennedy announced the goal of putting a man on the Moon before the end of the decade. In Kennedy's vision, space was the next great frontier for humankind. It was easy to imagine that a mission to the Moon could be the preliminary step that would eventually lead to a base on the Moon.

To prepare for a lunar expedition, NASA mobilized a workforce of over 400,000 from universities, industry, and technical centres to develop the necessary science and technology. The government poured over $25 billion—well over $130 billion in 21st century value—into the enterprise. The result was Project Gemini, which consisted of two-man crews testing new equipment and maneuvers. During the ten manned flights, completed between 1965 and 1966, the Gemini crews undertook space walks and rendezvoused with another spacecraft. New equipment, such as fuel cells and computers, were introduced.

In 1967, the Soviets tested the Soyuz, a new spacecraft they planned to use in their own lunar mission. The Soyuz lunar project was eventually canceled, but modern versions of the spacecraft are used today to carry people and supplies to the International Space Station.

After Gemini came the Apollo program, which required the development of two new spacecraft and more powerful rockets. The Apollo program received more public and government support than any manned space enterprise in American history. The first mission, Apollo 1, ended tragically in 1967 when the three-man crew was killed in a fire during a preflight test. Spectacular successes followed, however, with the first manned Apollo mission and then the first lunar orbit, Apollo 8. During that 1968 mission, astronaut Williams Anders took the famous photograph of Earth rising over the edge of the Moon.

Neil Armstrong's "one small step for [a] man" left a footprint, but it was what the lunar landing signified for future manned space missions that left a true lasting impression. Getty Images

In July 1969, Kennedy's pledge to put a man on the Moon came to fruition. Six hundred million people watched the rocket launch on television. Three days later, Neil Armstrong and Buzz Aldrin piloted the lunar module *Eagle* to the surface of the Moon. After years spent developing technology and expertise, the crew aboard Apollo 11 made history when Neil Armstrong stepped onto the Moon's surface. The lunar landing is widely regarded as the most iconic success of the NASA space program. Perhaps more important, the landing is also one of the prime historic moments of the 20th century.

Five more Apollo missions to the Moon followed, ending with Apollo 17 touching down in 1972. Astronauts made Moon walks, explored the Moon's surface with the lunar rover, and collected samples. By this time America's space pioneers were world famous.

Everybody knew the names of Alan Shepard, Gus Grissom, John Glenn, Buzz Aldrin, and many other astronauts.

After the lunar missions ended, public interest faded and funding for the space program diminished. The political climate was changing. The space race had ended, and tensions between the United States and the U.S.S.R. abated for a period during the mid-1970s. Issues such as the Vietnam War and economic concerns overtook the Cold War in the public eye. Space exploration projects grew less ambitious, and budget considerations became a greater factor.

The 1970s saw the beginning of increased international cooperation in space exploration. Pooling their resources, former adversaries the United States and the U.S.S.R. conducted a joint Apollo-Soyuz space mission in 1975. That year also saw the formation of the European Space Agency. In 1976, the U.S.S.R. took the first "guest cosmonauts" from other countries into space.

In the 1980s, the United States hosted foreign astronauts on the space shuttle, a program approved in 1972 by the Nixon administration. Previous spacecraft had been throwaways, meaning they could be used on one mission only. The space shuttle was designed as a reusable craft that could ferry up to eight astronauts back and forth from space. The shuttle's promoters claimed that it would make travel into space a routine and relatively inexpensive venture—projections that would later prove to be wildly optimistic.

Nine years after the initiation of the project, the first space shuttle took flight. There have been five space shuttles used in a variety of space missions: *Columbia, Challenger, Discovery, Endeavour,* and *Atlantis.* The shuttle program suffered a serious setback in 1986, when *Challenger* exploded shortly after liftoff, killing all seven astronauts aboard. It was the worst disaster of NASA's history. In 2003, there was an eerie feeling of déjà vu as *Columbia* disintegrated upon reentry after completing a successful mission, claiming the lives of another seven-member crew. Despite the second disaster, the remaining shuttles returned to space, but the shuttle's effectiveness was soon called into question. NASA has scheduled the retirement of the space shuttle program for 2010.

Cooperation with the Russians and spacecraft design were not the only changes the American space program was undergoing. In addition, the astronaut corps has also become much more diverse since the early days. The first Project Mercury astronauts were

The countdown to liftoff is just as thrilling today as it was in the early days of manned spaceflight. AFP/Getty Images

chosen for their abilities as pilots and physical fitness. During the mid-1960s, scientists were selected for astronaut training for the first time. Sally Ride became the first American woman in space in 1983.

Space travel had moved beyond trips to the Moon as well. Long before established space programs had become a reality, visionaries such as the rocket pioneer Wernher von Braun and others had conceived of space stations that could serve as way stations for astronauts traveling about the solar system. Manned missions have not achieved that level of exploration, but humans have built a number of space stations.

Precursors to today's space stations began in 1971, when the Soviets launched a series of Salyut space stations with living space for several cosmonauts. In 1973, the United States launched a space station called Skylab, and three different crews spent time aboard before it was abandoned the next year. The Soviet space station Mir, launched in 1986, hosted 104 crew members from 12 countries before being jettisoned in 2001. Construction of its successor, the International Space Station—which is a cooperative venture of 16 countries—began in 1998.

Even as astronauts accomplish new feats and future missions are planned, many people question whether manned space exploration is worth the cost in terms of money and risk to human lives. Would NASA's $15 billion budget be better spent on social programs that would help people directly?

In 1962, President Kennedy invoked patriotism and the potential for progress in justifying his space program:

Our leadership in science and in industry, our hopes for peace and security, our obligations to ourselves as well as others, all require us to make this effort, to solve these mysteries, to solve them for the good of all men, and to become the world's leading space-faring nation. We set sail on this new sea because there is new knowledge to be gained, and new rights to be won, and they must be won and used for the progress of all people . . . The growth of our science and education will be enriched by new knowledge of our universe and environment, by new techniques of learning and mapping and observation, by new tools and computers for industry, medicine, the home as well as the school.

Kennedy was correct in his predictions of technology transfer, whereby the application of technology developed for the space program could be used for non-space purposes. In addition, NASA's budget is reinvested in the American economy since much of it goes to pay the scientists, engineers, and other workers involved in the space program. Some of the additional benefits of space exploration, such as the inspiration it has provided for generations of schoolchildren, cannot be measured in terms of money.

What does the future hold for manned spaceflight? Construction and research on the International Space Station will continue. Space tourists paying millions of dollars for a trip to the space station is a trend that is likely to expand. The United States will unveil a successor to the space shuttle, and a return to the Moon, as well as expeditions to Mars, are in the offing. From there, no one can say for certain what the future of manned spaceflight will encompass. After all, as this book illustrates, space is a limitless frontier that holds the potential to defy all predictions.

CHAPTER 1

PRECURSORS IN FICTION AND FACT

S ince ancient times, people around the world have studied the heavens and used their observations and explanations of astronomical phenomena for both religious and practical purposes. Some dreamed of leaving Earth to explore other worlds. For example, the French satirist Cyrano de Bergerac in the 17th century wrote *Histoire comique des états et empires de la lune* (1656) and *Histoire comique des états et empires du soleil* (1662; together in English as *A Voyage to the Moon: With Some Account of the Solar World*, 1754), describing fictional journeys to the Moon and the Sun. Two centuries later, the French author Jules Verne and the English novelist and historian H.G. Wells infused their stories with descriptions of outer space and of spaceflight that were consistent with the best understanding of the time. Verne's *De la Terre à la Lune* (1865; *From the Earth to the Moon*) and Wells's *The War of the Worlds* (1898) and *The First Men in the Moon* (1901) used sound scientific principles to describe space travel and encounters with alien beings.

In order to translate these fictional images of space travel into reality, it was necessary to devise some practical means of countering the influence of Earth's gravity. By the beginning of the 20th century, the centuries-old technology of rockets had advanced to the point at which it was reasonable to consider their use to accelerate objects to a velocity sufficient to enter orbit around Earth or even to escape Earth's gravity and travel away from the planet.

PIONEERS

The first person to study in detail the use of rockets for spaceflight was the Russian schoolteacher and mathematician Konstantin Tsiolkovsky. In 1903 his article "Exploration of Cosmic Space by Means of Reaction Devices" laid out many of the principles of spaceflight. Up to his death in 1935, Tsiolkovsky continued to publish sophisticated studies on the theoretical aspects of spaceflight. He never complemented his writings with practical experiments in rocketry, but his work greatly influenced later space and rocket research in the Soviet Union and Europe.

Rocketry pioneer Hermann Oberth was by birth a Romanian but by nationality a German. Reading Verne's *From the Earth to the Moon* as a youth inspired him to study the requirements for interplanetary travel. Oberth's 1922 doctoral dissertation on rocket-powered flight was rejected by the University of Heidelberg for being too speculative, but it became the basis for his classic 1923 book *Die Rakete zu den Planetenräumen* ("The Rocket into Interplanetary Space"). The work explained the mathematical theory of rocketry, applied the theory to rocket design, and discussed the possibility of constructing space stations and of traveling to other planets.

In 1929 Oberth published a second influential book, *Wege Zur Raumschiffahrt* (*Ways to Spaceflight*). His works led to the creation of a number of rocket clubs in Germany as enthusiasts tried to turn Oberth's ideas into practical devices. The most important of these groups historically was the Verein für Raumschiffahrt (VfR; "Society for Spaceship Travel"), which had as a member the young Wernher von Braun, who played a prominent role in all aspects of rocketry and space exploration, first in Germany and, after World War II, in the United States.

Although his work was crucial in stimulating the development of rocketry in Germany, Oberth himself had only a limited role in that development. Alone among the rocket pioneers, Oberth lived to see his ideas become reality. He was a guest of honour at the July 16, 1969, launch of Apollo 11.

Although Tsiolkovsky, Oberth, and American professor and inventor Robert Goddard are recognized as the most influential of the first-generation space pioneers, others made contributions in the early decades of the 20th century. For example, the Frenchman Robert Esnault-Pelterie began work on the theoretical aspects of spaceflight as early as 1907 and subsequently published several major books on the topic. He, like Tsiolkovsky in the Soviet Union and Oberth in Germany, was an effective publicist regarding the potential of space exploration.

In Austria, Eugen Sänger worked on rocket engines. In the late 1920s, he proposed developing a "rocket plane" that could reach a speed exceeding 10,000 km (more than 6,000 miles) per hour and an altitude of more than 65 km (40 miles). Interested in Sänger's work,

ROBERT HUTCHINGS GODDARD

In the United States, pioneering work in rocket science was performed by Robert Hutchings Goddard, an American professor and inventor who is generally acknowledged to be the father of modern rocketry.

Born in Worcester, Mass., on Oct. 5, 1882, Goddard was the only child of a family of modest means. From childhood on he displayed great curiosity about physical phenomena and a bent toward inventiveness. In 1898 young Goddard's imagination was fired by H.G. Wells' novel War of the Worlds. *Shortly thereafter, as he recounted, he actually dreamed of constructing a workable spaceflight machine. On Oct. 19, 1899, a day that became his "Anniversary Day," he climbed a cherry tree in his backyard and ". . . imagined how wonderful it would be to make some device which had even the possibility of ascending to Mars . . . when I descended the tree . . . existence at last seemed very purposive."*

Goddard's fascination with spaceflight continued into his college years at the Worcester Polytechnic Institute. Later, in 1908, he began a long association with Clark University, Worcester, where he earned his doctorate, taught physics, and carried out rocket experiments. He was the first to prove that thrust and consequent propulsion can take place in a vacuum, needing no air to push against. He was the first to explore mathematically the ratios of energy and thrust per weight of various fuels, including liquid oxygen and liquid hydrogen. He was also the first to develop a rocket motor using liquid fuels (liquid oxygen and gasoline). In a small structure adjoining his laboratory, a liquid-propelled rocket in a static test in 1925 "operated satisfactorily and lifted its own weight," he wrote.

On March 16, 1926, the world's first flight of a liquid-propelled rocket engine took place on his Aunt Effie's farm in Auburn, Mass., achieving a brief liftoff. In achieving liftoff of his small but sophisticated rocket engine, Goddard carried his experiments further than Tsiolkovsky and Oberth.

Goddard died of throat cancer in 1945, at the threshold of the age of jet and rocket. Years later, his work was acknowledged by the United States government when a $1 million settlement was made for the use of his patents.

Nazi Germany in 1936 invited him to continue his investigations in that country.

EARLY ROCKET DEVELOPMENT

Rocketry went from a largely theoretical discipline to practical applications with the advent of large-scale experimentation that occurred in the 1930s and 40s. Germany, Russia, and the United States were at the forefront of rocket development at this time. The quest to conquer space was not the only motivating factor for these countries, however. As tensions that would inexorably lead the world into war increased, nations looked to burgeoning rocket technology as a delivery method for advanced weaponry.

GERMANY

It was space exploration that motivated the members of the German VfR to build their rockets, but in the early 1930s their work came to the attention of the German military. At that time Capt. Walter R. Dornberger (later major general) was in charge of solid-fuel rocket research and development in the Ordnance Department of Germany's 100,000-man armed forces, the Reichswehr. He recognized the military potential of liquid-fueled rockets and the ability of Braun. Dornberger arranged a research grant from the Ordnance Department for Braun, who then did research at a small development station that was set up adjacent to Dornberger's existing solid-fuel rocket test facility at the Kummersdorf Army Proving Grounds near Berlin. Two years later Braun received a Ph.D. in physics from the University of Berlin. His thesis, which, for reasons of military security, bore the nondescript title "About Combustion Tests," contained the theoretical investigation and developmental experiments on 300- and 660-pound-thrust (1,335 to 2,937 newtons) rocket engines.

By December 1934 Braun's group, which then included one additional engineer and three mechanics, had successfully launched two rockets that rose vertically to more than 1.5 miles (2.4 km). But by this time there was no longer a

Test launch of a V-2 rocket. Camera Press

German rocket society; rocket tests had been forbidden by decree, and the only way open to such research was through the military forces.

To give Braun's engineers the needed space and secrecy for their work, the German government erected a development and test centre at Peenemünde on the coast of the Baltic Sea. Dornberger was the military commander and Braun was the technical director.

There they developed, among other devices, the V-2 (meaning Vengeance Weapon 2 but originally designated the

A-4) ballistic missile. The V-2 was 14 metres (47 feet) long, weighed 12,700–13,200 kg (28,000–29,000 pounds) at launching, and developed about 60,000 pounds of thrust (267,000 newtons), burning alcohol and liquid oxygen. The payload was about 725 kg (1,600 pounds) of high explosive, horizontal range was about 320 km (200 miles), and the peak altitude usually reached was roughly 80 km (50 miles). It was first launched successfully on Oct. 3, 1942, and was fired against Paris on Sept. 6, 1944. Two days later the first of more than 1,100 V-2s was fired against Great Britain (the last on March 27, 1945). Belgium was also heavily bombarded.

Although built as a weapon of war, the V-2 later served as the predecessor of many of the rockets used in the early space programs of the United States and the Soviet Union. As World War II neared its end in early 1945, Braun, his younger brother Magnus, Dornberger, and the entire German rocket development team chose to surrender to the United States, where they believed they would likely receive support for their rocket research and space exploration plans. Later in the year, they were taken to the United States, as were their engineering plans and the parts needed to construct a number of V-2s. The German rocket team played a central role in the early development of space launchers for the United States.

In later years, Braun attempted to justify his involvement in the development of the German V-2 rocket and stated that patriotic motives outweighed whatever qualms he had about the moral implications of his nation's policies under Hitler. He also emphasized the innate impartiality of scientific research, which in itself has no moral dimensions until its products are put to use by the larger society.

UNITED STATES

In 1936, as Braun was developing rockets for the German military, several young American engineers led by graduate student Frank Malina began working on rocketry at the Guggenheim Aeronautical Laboratory of the California Institute of Technology (GALCIT). Malina's group was supported by the eminent aerodynamicist Theodore von Kármán, GALCIT's director, and it included Chinese engineer Qian Xuesen (Ch'ien Hsüeh-sen), who in the 1950s returned home to become one of the pioneers of rocketry in China.

In 1943 Malina and his associates began calling their group the Jet Propulsion Laboratory (JPL), a name that was formally adopted the following year. JPL soon became a centre for missile research and development for the U.S. Army. Following World War II, those weapons were adapted for use in early U.S. space experiments. After 1958, when it became part of the newly established National Aeronautics and Space Administration (NASA), JPL adapted itself to being the leading U.S. centre for solar system exploration.

Goddard's early tests were modestly financed over a period of several years by the Smithsonian Institution. In 1929, following an aborted and noisy flight test that brought unwanted press notice to the publicity-shy inventor, Charles A. Lindbergh was instrumental in procuring funding for Goddard's experiments. From 1930 to the mid-1940s, the Guggenheim Fund for the Promotion of Aeronautics financed the work on a scale that made possible a small shop and crew and experimental flights at Roswell, N.M.

At Roswell, Goddard became the first to shoot a liquid-fuel rocket faster than the speed of sound (1935). He obtained the first patents of a steering apparatus for the rocket machine and of the use of "step rockets" to gain great altitudes. He also developed the first pumps suitable for rocket fuels and self-cooling rocket motors. However, news of his work drew from the press and the public high amusement that "Moony" Goddard could take seriously the possibility of travel beyond Earth. His small rockets, early prototypes of modern thrusters, achieved altitudes of up to 1.6 km (1 mile) above the prairie.

During World War II, Goddard offered his work to the military, but lack of interest led to his closing down the Roswell establishment. However, Lindbergh and the Guggenheim Fund remained staunch advocates of Goddard and the feasibility of space exploration.

SOVIET UNION

In the U.S.S.R., the government took an interest in rockets as early as 1921 with the founding of a military facility devoted to rocket research. Over the next decade, that centre was expanded and renamed the Gas Dynamics Laboratory. There in the early 1930s, Valentin Glushko carried out pioneering work on rocket engines.

Meanwhile, other rocket enthusiasts in the Soviet Union organized into societies that by 1931 had consolidated into an organization known as GIRD (the abbreviation in Russian for "Group for the Study of Reactive Motion"), with branches in Moscow and Leningrad. Emerging as leaders of the Moscow branch were the aeronautical engineer Sergey Korolyov, who had become interested in spaceflight at a young age, and the early space visionary Fridrikh Tsander. Korolyov and a colleague, Mikhail Tikhonravov, on Aug. 17, 1933, launched the first Soviet liquid-fueled rocket. Later that year, the Moscow and Leningrad branches of GIRD were combined with the Gas Dynamics Laboratory to form the military-controlled Rocket Propulsion Research Institute (RNII), which five years later became Scientific-Research Institute 3 (NII-3). In its early years, the organization did not work directly on space technology, but ultimately it played a central role in Soviet rocket development.

Korolyov was arrested in 1937 as part of the Soviet leader Joseph Stalin's great purges of intellectuals and was sent to a Siberian prison. After Stalin recognized the imprudence of removing the best technical people from the Soviet war effort, Korolyov was transferred to a prison-based design bureau, where he spent most of World War II working on weapons, although not on large rockets.

By the end of the war, Stalin had become interested in ballistic missiles, and he sent a team, which included Korolyov, on visits to Germany to investigate the V-2 program. A number of German engineers were relocated to the Soviet Union in the aftermath of the war, but they did not play a central role in postwar Soviet rocket development; most returned to Germany in the early 1950s.

PREPARING FOR SPACEFLIGHT

Between 1946 and 1951 Braun and about 100 members of his group conducted test firings of captured German V-2 rockets at the U.S. Army Ordnance Corps test site at White Sands, N.M. These sounding-rocket flights reached high altitudes (120–200 km [75–125 miles]) before falling back to Earth. Although the primary purpose of the tests was to advance rocket technology, the army invited American scientists interested in high-altitude research to put experiments aboard the V-2s. An Upper Atmosphere Research Panel, chaired by the physicist James Van Allen, was formed to coordinate the scientific use of these rocket launchings.

The panel had a central role in the early years of American space science, which focused on experiments on solar and stellar ultraviolet radiation, the aurora, and the nature of the upper atmosphere. As the supply of V-2s dwindled, other U.S.-built sounding rockets such as the WAC Corporal, Aerobee, and Viking were put into use. In other countries,

particularly the Soviet Union, rocket-based upper-atmosphere research also took place after World War II.

In the early 1950s, scientists began planning a coordinated international investigation of Earth, to be called the International Geophysical Year (IGY), that would be held in 1957–58 under the auspices of the International Council of Scientific Unions. By this time, progress in rocket development had advanced such that orbiting of an artificial satellite around Earth by 1957 seemed feasible. At the urging of American scientists, IGY planners in 1954 called for scientifically instrumented satellites to be launched as part of IGY activities. Soon thereafter, the governments of the Soviet Union and the United States each announced plans to do so.

In the years following World War II, the United States and the U.S.S.R. became political and military competitors in what soon was being called the Cold War. Because the Soviet Union was a closed society, U.S. leaders gave high priority to developing technology that could help gather intelligence on military preparations within the Soviet borders. As orbiting satellites neared realization, the idea of equipping such satellites with cameras and flying them over Soviet territory became more attractive to U.S. planners, and the U.S. Air Force began work on a reconnaissance satellite project.

Still unresolved, however, was the question of whether it would violate national sovereignty to fly over a country's territory in orbit, above most of the atmosphere.

One reason the U.S. government had committed itself to the IGY satellite program was that it wanted to establish the principle that outer space was not subject to claims of territorial sovereignty and thus that an orbiting satellite could pass freely over any point on Earth. Such overflights were essential if reconnaissance satellites were to have intelligence value.

As scientific and military planners contemplated initial space projects and engineers worked on developing the needed launch vehicles, the idea that humans would soon begin the exploration of space entered popular imagination. In Europe, since the 1930s, the British Interplanetary Society had been actively promoting the idea that human space travel was soon to happen. American movies such as *The Day the Earth Stood Still* (1950), *Destination Moon* (1950), and *When Worlds Collide* (1951) contained vivid images of such journeys. Reports were widespread of sightings of unidentified flying objects (UFOs), which were thought by some to be spacecraft from alien worlds.

Authors such as Isaac Asimov, Robert A. Heinlein, and Arthur C. Clarke both discussed the reality of space technology in popular writings and constructed believable science-fiction stories based on its use. A central figure in popularization efforts within the United States was Braun, who had become chief of the U.S. Army ballistic-weapon program. (Under his leadership, the Redstone, Jupiter-C, Juno, and Pershing missiles were developed.) A charismatic spokesman for the idea of space travel, Braun, in a series of talks, books, magazine articles, and television appearances during the 1950s, reached millions of people with his ideas for establishing orbiting space stations and human travel to the Moon and Mars. The efforts of Braun and other popularizers helped create a receptive climate for initial government proposals to undertake space activities and, particularly, to put humans in space.

Frank Malina, a cofounder of the Jet Propulsion Laboratory, pictured with an early model of the WAC Corporal research rocket. The surrounding steelwork is the lower section of the vertical launch tower. NASA/JPL

CHAPTER 2

SPACEFLIGHT BEGINS

Although Soviet plans to orbit a satellite during the IGY had been discussed extensively in technical circles, the Oct. 4, 1957, launch of Sputnik 1 came as a surprise, and even a shock, to most people. Prior to the launch, skepticism had been widespread about the U.S.S.R.'s technical capabilities to develop both a sophisticated scientific satellite and a rocket powerful enough to put it into orbit.

Under Korolyov's direction, however, the Soviet Union had been building an intercontinental ballistic missile (ICBM), with engines designed by Glushko, that was capable of delivering a heavy nuclear warhead to American targets. That ICBM, called the R-7 or Semyorka ("Number 7"), was first successfully tested on Aug. 21, 1957, which cleared the way for its use to launch a satellite. Fearing that development of the elaborate scientific satellite intended as the Soviet IGY contribution would keep the U.S.S.R. from being the first into space, Korolyov and his associates, particularly Tikhonravov, designed a much simpler 83.6-kg (184-pound) sphere carrying only two radio transmitters and four antennas. After the success of the R-7 in August, that satellite was rushed into production and became Sputnik 1.

A second, larger satellite carrying scientific instruments and a dog named Laika, the first living creature in orbit, was launched November 3. The even larger, instrumented spacecraft originally intended to be the first Soviet satellite went into orbit in May 1958 as Sputnik 3.

Sputnik 3, the first multipurpose space-science satellite placed in orbit. Launched May 15, 1958, by the Soviet Union, it made and transmitted measurements of the pressure and composition of Earth's upper atmosphere, the concentration of charged particles, and the influx of primary cosmic rays. Tass/Sovfoto

After President Eisenhower, in May 1955, had committed the United States to an IGY satellite, the army, navy, and air force competed for the assignment. (No civilian organization existed that was capable of developing the launch vehicle needed.) The mission was assigned to the Naval Research Laboratory, rather than to the army's Redstone Arsenal, where Braun worked, so that the work would not interfere with Redstone's higher-priority development of ballistic missiles.

The navy project, called Vanguard, would use a new launch vehicle based on modified Viking and Aerobee sounding rockets to orbit a small scientific satellite. Vanguard made slow progress over the subsequent two years, but, after Sputnik's success, the White House pressed to have the satellite launched as quickly as possible. On Dec. 6, 1957, the Vanguard rocket rose only slightly off its launch pad before exploding and sending the satellite not into orbit but onto a Florida beach.

Braun and his army superiors had not agreed with the decision to assign the satellite mission to the navy. After the launches of the first two Sputniks, they secured permission to attempt their own satellite launch. In anticipation of such a situation, they had kept in touch with JPL and Van Allen and so were able to prepare a satellite quickly. On Jan. 31, 1958, Braun's Jupiter-C launch vehicle, a modified Redstone ballistic missile, carried into orbit Explorer 1, the first U.S. satellite. Designed at JPL, Explorer 1 carried Van Allen's experiment to measure cosmic rays. The results from this experiment and similar ones aboard other U.S. and Soviet satellites launched that same year revealed that Earth was surrounded by two zones of radiation, now known as the Van Allen radiation belts, comprising energetic particles trapped by Earth's magnetic field.

Initial satellite launches were scientific in character, but U.S. government interest in reconnaissance satellites persisted. In February 1958, President Eisenhower authorized the development, under conditions of great secrecy, of such a spacecraft. The project, which came to be called Corona, would take pictures over

the Soviet Union and return them to Earth by dropping the exposed film in a capsule that would be snatched out of the air as it parachuted back from space. After 12 failures, the first successful Corona mission took place on Aug. 18, 1960; the returned film contained images of many previously unknown Soviet airfields and missile sites.

NASA AND U.S. MILITARY SPACE AGENCIES

As part of its response to the first Sputnik launches, the United States government debated how best to organize itself for its space activities. At the time, the military services, particularly the air force and the army, hoped that they would have a leading role in space. As an alternative to this rivalry between the services, President Eisenhower in February 1958 created the Defense Advanced Research Projects Agency (DARPA) and assigned it responsibility for all U.S. space projects. Soon afterward, he decided to separate civilian from military space efforts and proposed the creation of a National Aeronautics and Space Administration (NASA) to manage the civilian segment.

After approval by Congress, NASA began operation on Oct. 1, 1958. DARPA was not successful in establishing itself as a military space agency. By 1960, after the army had been obliged to relinquish control of JPL and Braun's rocket team to NASA management, the air force had emerged as the leading military service for space.

Eisenhower also decided to create a separate organization to manage the secret reconnaissance satellite program. This effort resulted in the National Reconnaissance Office (NRO), jointly directed by the Department of Defense and the Central Intelligence Agency. The very existence of this organization was kept secret until 1992. The NRO operated the initial Corona program until 1972. It continued to manage the development of successor photointelligence satellite systems of increasing technological sophistication and also developed radar-surveillance and electronic-signals-collection satellites. All were operated under conditions of the highest secrecy.

After it received its mandate to send Americans to the Moon, NASA grew into a large organization. From its headquarters in Washington, D.C., it operated 10 field centres established throughout the United States to carry out research and technology development and to manage the various universities and industrial contractors involved in the U.S. civilian space program. At the peak of the Apollo program, NASA had 34,000 employees; by the end of the

(From left) *William H. Pickering, James Van Allen, and Wernher von Braun triumphantly raising a full-size model of the first U.S. satellite, Explorer 1, at a press conference following the craft's launch on Jan. 31, 1958. A small model of the Jupiter-C launch vehicle stands on a table in front of Braun.* NASA/JPL

20th century, this labour force had shrunk to 19,000, but NASA remained by far the largest space agency in the world.

The air force had no separate organization for space until 1982, when the U.S. Air Force Space Command was created to manage its military space operations, which involved the use of satellites for meteorology, communication, navigation, and early warning of missile attack. The other U.S. military services soon created similar organizations to administer their smaller space activities. In 1985 these organizations were brought under a unified U.S. Space Command, dominated by the air force, which was responsible for 85 percent of military space activities. Research and development efforts related to military space programs were managed by various government laboratories and carried out primarily by American industry.

THE SPACE RACE BEGINS

During the 1950s, space planners in both the Soviet Union and the United States anticipated the launching of a human being into orbit as soon as the required launch vehicle and spacecraft could be developed and tested. Much of the initial thinking focused on some form of piloted space plane, which, after being launched atop a rocket, could maneuver in orbit and then return to Earth, gliding to a horizontal landing.

In the United States, the air force developed a rocket-powered experimental aircraft, the X-15, which, after being dropped from an in-flight B-52 bomber, could reach

North American Aviation X-15 rocket-powered plane being air-launched from a Boeing B-52 bomber. Flights of the experimental X-15 in the 1960s set unofficial altitude and speed records for piloted aircraft and contributed to the development of the U.S. manned spaceflight program. NASA

altitudes as high as 108 km (67 miles), the edge of outer space. Nevertheless, the X-15 could not achieve the velocity and altitude needed for orbital flight. That was the mission of Dyna-Soar, another air force project. Dyna-Soar was to be a piloted reusable delta-winged vehicle that would be launched into orbit by a modified Titan ICBM and could carry out either bombing or reconnaissance missions over the Soviet Union or intercept a Soviet satellite in orbit. Although a full-scale vehicle was built and six people were chosen to train as Dyna-Soar crew, the project was canceled in 1963.

Rather than base their human spaceflight programs on space planes, the Soviet Union and the United States, in their desire to put people into space as quickly as possible, opted for a less technically demanding ballistic approach. A person would ride in a capsulelike spacecraft atop a rocket to achieve orbit. At the end of the flight, another rocket (called a retro-rocket) would slow down the spacecraft enough for it to fall back to Earth on a ballistic trajectory. To accomplish this feat, the spacecraft would have to survive the intense heat caused by reentering the atmosphere at a high speed and then carry its passenger safely back to Earth's surface. Informed by prior unmanned satellite launches and suborbital aircraft test flights, teams of engineers from both nations created the next generation of spacecraft.

VOSTOK

Soon after the success of the first Sputniks, Korolyov and his associate Tikhonravov began work on the design of an orbital spacecraft that could be used for two purposes. One was to conduct photo-reconnaissance missions and then return the exposed film to Earth. The other was to serve as a vehicle for the first human space-flight missions, in which a human being would replace the reconnaissance camera. The spacecraft was known as Object K, but it was called Vostok when it was used to carry a human into space.

Vostok had two sections—a spherical capsule in which the person would ride and a conical module that contained the instruments needed for its flight. The spacecraft was large for the time, weighing 4.73 metric tons. The crew capsule was completely covered by a thermal coating to protect it during reentry. Vostok was

designed so that the human aboard need not touch any control from launch to touchdown; he would be essentially just a passenger. Nor would he land with the spacecraft. Rather, he would be ejected from it at an altitude of 7 km (4.3 miles) and parachute to dry land, while the spacecraft landed nearby with its own parachutes.

The Soviet Union selected 20 air force pilots from 102 candidates for cosmonaut training in February 1960. These individuals also had to meet restrictions on height (170 cm, or 5 feet 7 inches) and weight (70 kg, or 154 pounds) because of the small size of the Soviet Vostok space-craft. The identity of these individuals was kept secret until they were actually launched into space. Most of the cosmonaut candidates were between 25 and 30 years old and thus did not have the extensive test pilot experience of their U.S. counterparts.

After a series of five test flights carrying dogs and human dummies, the first person lifted into space in Vostok 1 atop a modified R-7 rocket on April 12, 1961, from the Soviet launch site at the Baikonur Cosmodrome in Kazakhstan. The passenger, Yury Gagarin, who was by that time being called a cosmonaut, was a 27-year-old Russian test pilot. After firing of the retro-rocket 78 minutes into the mission, the crew capsule separated from the instrument module—although not without problems—and Gagarin parachuted to a soft landing 108 minutes after his launch. He had reported during the mission "I feel fine" and showed no ill effects from his one-orbit trip around the globe.

There were five additional one-person Vostok missions. In August 1961, Gherman Titov at age 25 (still the youngest person ever to fly in space) completed 17 orbits of Earth in Vostok 2. He became ill with space sickness (the equivalent of motion sickness on Earth) during the flight, an incident that caused a one-year delay in Vostok flights while Soviet physicians investigated the possibility that humans could not survive for extended times in the space environment. In August 1962, two Vostoks, 3 and 4, were orbited at the same time and came within 6.5 km (4 miles) of one another. This dual mission was repeated in June 1963; aboard the Vostok 6 spacecraft was Valentina Tereshkova, the first woman to fly in space.

MERCURY

The initial U.S. effort to launch a human into space was known as Project Mercury.

It was carried out by NASA, which had been given that responsibility over air force objections. NASA engineers, led by Robert Gilruth and Maxime Faget, designed a small cone-shaped capsule for the mission. Compared with the nearly five-metric-ton Vostok, it weighed 1.94 metric tons.

Unlike the Soviet approach, in which a cosmonaut was orbited on the first human spaceflight, NASA planned several suborbital test flights in which an astronaut would be in space for only a few minutes of his 15-minute up-and-down ride. Only after the Mercury equipment was checked and the effects of suborbital flight on the human body were measured would the United States commit to an orbital flight attempt. The Mercury capsule would parachute with its passenger all the way back to Earth's surface, to land in the ocean and be recovered by navy ships. Also in contrast to Vostok, the Mercury capsule was designed to allow

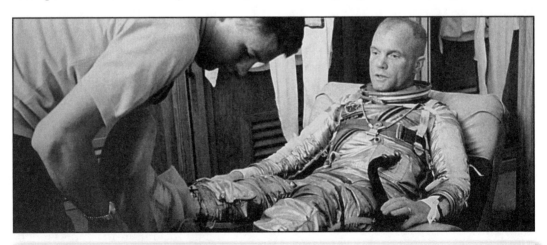

Mercury astronaut and American legend John Glenn gets suited up and briefed before an orbital flight in 1962. Getty Images

the astronaut to control some aspects of its flight while in space.

The first seven U.S. astronauts were chosen for Project Mercury in April 1959. They were selected from some 500 candidates, all members of the U.S. military. Each candidate was required to have experience as a pilot of high-performance jet aircraft and, because of the cramped conditions inside the Mercury spacecraft, to be no more than 5 feet 11 inches (180 cm) tall and weigh no more than 180 pounds (82 kg).

The United States used chimpanzees, rather than dogs, as test subjects prior to human flights. In what was intended to be the final test flight before a human launch, the chimpanzee Ham rode a suborbital trajectory on Jan. 31, 1961, using a Redstone rocket developed by Braun's team. Because the flight had experienced minor problems, Braun insisted on one more test flight with an unoccupied dummy spacecraft. If instead, as originally scheduled, that March 1961 flight had carried an astronaut, the United States would have been first with a human in space, although not in orbit. Alan B. Shepard, Jr., made the first manned Mercury flight atop a Redstone rocket on May 5, 1961. A second suborbital Mercury mission, carrying Virgil I. Grissom, followed in July.

John H. Glenn, Jr., became the first American astronaut to orbit Earth in his

Riding into space atop a modified Atlas intercontinental ballistic missile, Glenn became the first American to orbit Earth. NASA/Kennedy Space Center

three-orbit mission on Feb. 20, 1962. His Mercury spacecraft was launched by a modified air force Atlas ICBM. Three more one-man Mercury orbital flights, carrying astronauts M. Scott Carpenter, Walter M. Schirra, Jr., and L. Gordon Cooper, Jr., were conducted, the last being a 22-orbit mission in May 1963.

GEMINI AND VOSKHOD

In 1961 President Kennedy announced that the United States would send people to the Moon "before this decade is out." In order to test many of the techniques that would be needed to carry out a lunar mission, particularly rendezvousing and docking two objects in space, the United States in late 1961 decided to develop a two-person spacecraft called Gemini. The Gemini spacecraft was much more complex than the rudimentary Mercury capsule and, at 3.81 metric tons, was twice as heavy. Another converted air force ICBM, a Titan II, was used to launch the Gemini spacecraft.

The first manned Gemini mission, Gemini 3 with commander Virgil Grissom and pilot John Young, lifted into space on March 23, 1965. Nine more missions followed; the last, Gemini 12 with commander James Lovell and pilot Edwin "Buzz" Aldrin, was in November 1966. On the second mission, Gemini 4, in June 1965, Edward H. White II became the first American astronaut to operate outside a spacecraft. His 20-minute space walk—also known as extravehicular activity (EVA)—was without incident.

Although problems developed on many of the Gemini flights, the program demonstrated that people could live and work in space for as long as 14 days, more than the time needed for a round trip to the Moon. It also showed that astronauts could carry out rendezvous in space and could make useful observations of Earth, both visually and photographically.

As plans in the United States for multiple-astronaut missions became known, the Soviet Union worked to maintain its lead in the space race by modifying the Vostok spacecraft so that it could carry as many as three persons. Korolyov could accomplish this only by having the crew fly without wearing spacesuits. The redesigned spacecraft was known as Voskhod. There were two Voskhod missions, one with three people aboard in October 1964 and another with a two-man crew in March 1965. On the second mission, cosmonaut Aleksey Leonov became the first human to leave an orbiting spacecraft, less than three months before White. His 12-minute EVA was full of problems, and his reentry of the Voskhod spacecraft was particularly difficult.

SOYUZ

Korolyov and his associates began work in 1962 on a second-generation spacecraft, to be called Soyuz. The craft was to be capable not only of flights in Earth orbit but also, in modified versions, of flights around the Moon and even a lunar landing. The 7-metre- (23-foot-) long, 7-metric-ton vehicle comprises three

Russian Soyuz TM spacecraft (the mostly dark structure with extended solar panels) docked to a port on the Mir space station, in an image made from the U.S. space shuttle orbiter Atlantis, Sept. 21, 1996. NASA

modules joined in line—a central, bell-shaped descent module with contoured couches for as many as three persons during ascent, descent, and landing; a cylindrical service module mounted at the rear that provides propulsion, life support, and electrical power; and a spheroidal orbital module in front that carries the docking system and contains living facilities and cargo for the orbital phase of the mission. The three modules remain together throughout the mission until the spacecraft is deorbited; only the descent module returns to Earth intact.

The first launch of Soyuz, with a single cosmonaut, Vladimir Komarov, aboard, took place on April 23, 1967. Once the spacecraft reached orbit, it suffered a number of problems, which prompted ground controllers to bring Komarov back to Earth as soon as possible. After reentry, however, the spacecraft's main parachute did not fully deploy, and the Soyuz hit the ground at high speed. Komarov became the first person to perish during a space-flight, and the accident dealt a major blow to Soviet hopes of orbiting or landing on the Moon before the United States.

CHAPTER 3

THE RACE TO THE MOON

In the immediate aftermath of Gagarin's orbital flight, President Kennedy was advised by his vice president, Lyndon B. Johnson, of Braun's belief that the Soviet Union, using Korolyov's existing R-7 launcher, could well succeed in sending a multiperson spacecraft into Earth orbit and perhaps even around the Moon before the United States. The first competition that the United States had a good chance of winning would be that of a manned lunar landing, because it would require each country to develop a new, more powerful rocket. On those technical grounds and because a lunar landing would be a very visible demonstration of American strength, Kennedy announced on May 25, 1961, that the United States would commit itself to a lunar landing before 1970. At that time, only one American human spaceflight, Shepard's 15-minute suborbital journey, had been made.

In response to Kennedy's decision, the United States carried out a warlike, but peaceful, mobilization of financial and human resources. NASA's budget was increased almost 500 percent in three years, and at its peak the lunar landing program involved more than 34,000 NASA employees and 375,000 employees of industrial and university contractors.

By the end of 1962, the basic elements of what was called Project Apollo were in place. The launch vehicle would be a powerful Saturn V rocket, 110.6 metres (363 feet) tall and power-driven by five huge engines generating a total of 33,000 kilonewtons (7.5 million pounds) of lifting power at takeoff—100 times the takeoff thrust of the Redstone rocket that had launched Shepard.

After an intense debate, NASA chose a spacecraft configuration for Apollo that could be sent up in one launch, rather than a larger spacecraft that would need to be assembled in a series of rendezvous in Earth orbit. The Apollo spacecraft would have three sections. A Command Module would house the three-person crew on liftoff and landing and during the trip to and from the Moon. A Service Module would carry various equipment and the rocket engine needed to guide the spacecraft into lunar orbit and then send it back to Earth. A Lunar Module, comprising a descent stage and an ascent stage, would carry two people from lunar orbit to the Moon's surface and back to the Command Module. The ability of the Lunar Module's ascent stage to rendezvous and dock in lunar orbit with the Command Module after takeoff from the Moon was critical to the success of the mission. NASA also created a large new launch facility on Merritt Island, near Cape Canaveral, Fla., as the Apollo spaceport.

THE SOVIET RESPONSE

While committing the United States to winning the Moon race, President Kennedy also made several attempts in the early 1960s to convince the Soviet leadership that a cooperative lunar landing program between their two countries would be a better alternative. No positive reply from the Soviet Union was forthcoming, however. In fact, between 1961 and 1963, there was still vigorous debate within the Soviet Union over the wisdom of undertaking a lunar program, and no final decision had been made on the question.

Meanwhile, the separate design bureaus headed by Korolyov and his rival Vladimir Chelomey competed fiercely for a lunar mission assignment, either a flight around the Moon or an actual landing. Finally, in August 1964, Korolyov received the lunar landing assignment, and soon afterward Chelomey was given responsibility for planning a circumlunar flight to be carried out before the 50th anniversary of the Bolshevik Revolution, which would take place in October 1967. In 1965 Soviet leaders decided to combine the efforts of the two rivals for the circumlunar mission, using a version of Korolyov's Soyuz spacecraft and a new rocket, the UR-500 (also called the Proton), designed by Chelomey.

The rocket that Korolyov designed for the lunar landing effort was a five-stage vehicle called the N1. Like the Saturn V, it was huge, standing 112.8 metres (370 feet) tall and having a planned takeoff thrust of 44,500 kilonewtons (10 million pounds). Instead of a few large rocket engines in its first stage, however, the N1 had 30 smaller engines. These were developed by Nikolay Kuznetsov, an aircraft-engine chief designer who had little experience with rocket engines, rather than the more capable Glushko. Korolyov and Glushko, already personal adversaries for many years, had disagreed on the proper fuel for the N1, and they finally decided that they could no longer work together. Consequently, Korolyov turned to Kuznetsov, who chose the small-engine approach.

Indecision, inefficiencies, inadequate budgets, and personal and organizational rivalries in the Soviet system thus posed major obstacles to success in the race to the Moon. To these was added the unexpected death of Korolyov, age 59, during surgery on Jan. 14, 1966. This was a serious setback to the Soviet space program. Korolyov had been a charismatic leader and organizer. His successor, Vasily Mishin, attempted to maintain the program's momentum, but he was not the effective manager or politically sophisticated operator that Korolyov had been.

INTERIM DEVELOPMENTS

In the United States, Apollo moved forward as a high-priority program. A major setback occurred on Jan. 27, 1967, when astronauts Grissom, White, and Roger Chaffee were killed after their Apollo 1 Command Module caught fire during a ground test. The first manned Apollo mission, designated Apollo 7 and intended to test the redesigned Command Module, was launched into Earth orbit on Oct. 11, 1968. The launcher used was a Saturn IB, a less-powerful rocket than the Saturn V needed to reach the Moon.

The mission's success cleared the way for a bold step—the first launch of a crew atop a Saturn V to the lunar vicinity. On Dec. 21, 1968, the Apollo 8 Command and Service modules were put on a trajectory

Planet Earth rising above the lunar horizon, an awe-inspiring view captured in December 1968 by Apollo 8 astronauts as their orbit carried them clear of the far side of the Moon. NASA

that sent them into orbit around the Moon on Christmas Eve, December 24. The three astronauts—Frank Borman, James A. Lovell, Jr., and William A. Anders—sent back close-up images of the lunar surface, read from the biblical book of Genesis, and brought back vivid colour photographs of a blue planet Earth rising over the desolate lunar landscape. By the end of the mission, it was clear that the first lunar landing was only months away.

One reason for conducting the Apollo 8 mission was to allow NASA to test most of the systems needed for a lunar landing attempt while waiting to carry out a manned trial in Earth orbit of the Lunar Module, whose development was behind schedule. Another was the concern that the Soviet Union would beat the United States in sending people to the lunar vicinity. A circumlunar mission indeed had been part of Soviet plans, but the Soyuz 1 accident had made the October 1967 deadline infeasible.

Throughout 1968 a number of test flights of a circumlunar mission were made, using the Proton launcher and a version of the Soyuz spacecraft designated Zond. In September Zond 5 carried a biological payload, including two tortoises, around the Moon and safely back to Earth, but two months later the Zond 6 spacecraft depressurized and then crashed on landing, ending any hope for a quick follow-on launch with a human crew. Plans to send cosmonauts around the Moon in a Zond spacecraft were postponed indefinitely in March 1969, but two more scientifically successful unmanned circumlunar missions, Zond 7

and Zond 8, were carried out in 1969 and 1970, respectively.

The Soviet lunar landing program went forward rather fitfully after 1964. The missions were intended to employ the N1 launch vehicle and another variation of the Soyuz spacecraft, designated L3, that included a lunar landing module designed for one cosmonaut. Although an L3 spacecraft was constructed and three cosmonauts trained for its use, the N1 rocket was never successfully launched. After four failed attempts between 1969 and 1972—including a spectacular launch-pad explosion in July 1969—the N1 program was finally canceled in May 1974, and Soviet hopes for human missions to the Moon thus ended.

THE APOLLO LUNAR LANDINGS AND APOLLO-SOYUZ

By contrast with the Soviet lunar landing efforts, during 1969 all went well for the Apollo program. In March the Apollo 9 crew successfully tested the Lunar Module in Earth orbit, and in May the Apollo 10 crew carried out a full dress rehearsal for the landing, coming within 15,200 metres (50,000 feet) of the lunar surface. On July 16, 1969, astronauts Armstrong, Aldrin, and Michael Collins set off on the Apollo 11 mission, the first lunar landing attempt.

While Collins remained in lunar orbit in the Command Module, Armstrong piloted the Lunar Module, nicknamed Eagle, away from boulders on the lunar surface and to a successful landing on a flat lava plain called the Sea of Tranquillity

Apollo 11 astronaut Edwin Aldrin, photographed July 20, 1969, during the first manned mission to the Moon's surface. Reflected in Aldrin's faceplate is the Lunar Module and astronaut Neil Armstrong, who took the picture. NASA

The far side of the Moon, photographed during the Apollo 11 mission, 1969. NASA

at 4:18 PM U.S. Eastern Daylight Time on July 20. He reported to mission control, "Houston. Tranquillity Base here. The Eagle has landed." Six and a half hours later, Armstrong, soon followed by Aldrin, left the Lunar Module and took the first human step on the surface of another celestial body. As he did so, he noted, "That's one small step for [a] man, one giant leap for mankind." (In the excitement of the moment, Armstrong skipped the "a" in the statement he had prepared.)

Concluding 2.5 hours of activity on the lunar surface, the two men returned to the Lunar Module with 21.7 kg (47.8 pounds) of lunar samples. Twelve hours later, they blasted off the Moon in the Lunar Module's ascent stage and rejoined Collins in the Command Module. The crew returned to Earth on July 24, splashing down in the Pacific Ocean.

The successful Apollo 12 mission followed in November 1969. The Apollo 13 mission, launched in April 1970, experienced an explosion of the oxygen tank in its Service Module on the outbound trip to the Moon. The crew survived this accident only through the improvised use of the Lunar Module as living quarters in order to preserve the remaining capabilities of the Command Module for

Apollo 15 astronaut James B. Irwin standing in back of the Lunar Roving Vehicle; the Lunar Module (LM) is at left with the modular equipment storage assembly (MESA) in front of it. NASA

Apollo 15 spacecraft as it lifts off from Cape Kennedy, Florida, U.S., atop a Saturn V three-stage rocket, July 26, 1971. A camera mounted at the mobile launch tower's 110-metre (360-foot) level recorded this photograph. NASA

reentering Earth's atmosphere after they had returned from their circumlunar journey. Four more Apollo missions followed. On each of the final three, the crew had a small cartlike rover that allowed them to travel several kilometres from their landing site. The final mission, Apollo 17, which

was conducted in December 1972, included geologist Harrison Schmitt, the only trained scientist to set foot on the Moon.

The United States had won the race to the Moon, but that race had been motivated primarily by political considerations. After the early 1970s there was no interest within the U.S. government for the next three decades in additional lunar exploration or in sending people to Mars or any other distant destination. No human has traveled beyond near-Earth orbit since Apollo 17.

An Apollo spacecraft was used for the last time in 1975. Three years earlier, as a sign of improved U.S.-Soviet relations, the two countries had agreed to carry out a joint mission in which an Apollo spacecraft carrying three astronauts would dock in orbit with a Soyuz vehicle having two cosmonauts aboard. The Apollo-Soyuz

Earth rises in the distance as Apollo 17 astronaut Harrison Schmitt admires a U.S. flag planted in the Moon's surface. Getty Images

Test Project, which took place in July 1975, featured a "handshake in space" between Apollo commander Thomas P. Stafford and Soyuz commander Aleksey Leonov.

SCIENTIFIC RESULTS FROM APOLLO

The Apollo program revolutionized human understanding of the Moon. The samples collected and the human and instrumental observations have continued to be studied into the 21st century. Analyses of samples from the Luna missions have continued as well and are valuable because they were collected from eastern equatorial areas far from the Apollo sites.

One new and fundamental result has come from radiometric age dating of the samples. When a rock cools from the molten to the solid state, its radioactive isotopes are immobilized in mineral crystal lattices and then decay in place. Knowing the rate of decay of one nuclear species (nuclide) into another, scientists can, in principle, use the ratios of decay products as a clock to measure the time elapsed since the rock cooled. Some nuclides, such as isotopes of rubidium and strontium, can be used to date rocks that are billions of years old.

The required measurements are threatened by contamination and other problems, such as past events that might have reset the clock. Nevertheless, with great care in sample preparation and mass spectrometry techniques, the isotopic ratios can be found and converted into age estimates. By the time of the Apollo sample returns, scientists had refined this art, and, using meteorite samples, they were already investigating the early history of the solar system.

Analysis of the first lunar samples confirmed that the Moon is an evolved body with a long history of differentiation and volcanic activity. Unlike the crust of Earth, however, the lunar crust is not recycled by tectonic processes, so it has preserved the records of ancient events. Highland rock samples returned by the later Apollo missions are nearly four billion years old, revealing that the Moon's crust was already solid soon after the planets condensed out of the solar nebula. The mare basalts, though they cover a wide range of ages, generally show that the basin-filling volcanic outpourings occurred long after the formation of the highlands; this is the reason they are believed to have originated from later radioactive heating within the

SATURN

Saturn was a series of three large two- and three-stage vehicles for launching spacecraft, developed by the United States beginning in 1958 in connection with the manned Apollo Moon-landing program. Saturn I, the first U.S. rocket specifically developed for spaceflight, was a two-stage, liquid-fuel vehicle that placed unmanned test versions of Apollo spacecraft and other satellites into Earth orbit in the early 1960s. The first firing, on Oct. 27, 1961, was followed by nine more successful launches. An upgraded version, the Saturn IB, was used for unmanned and manned Apollo Earth-orbital missions (1966–68) and subsequently for carrying crews to the first U.S. space station, Skylab (1973), and for the U.S.-Soviet Apollo-Soyuz Test Project (1975).

Saturn V, a three-stage vehicle, was designed for manned Apollo lunar flights. The first Saturn V was launched on Nov. 9, 1967. It was employed for 10 U.S. manned Apollo missions (Apollo 8–17, 1968–72) and a final time, unmanned, in 1973 to orbit Skylab. In taking the three-module Apollo spacecraft and crew to the Moon, the Saturn V's first stage, powered by five large kerosene–liquid-oxygen engines and weighing more than 2,000,000 kg (4,400,000 pounds) fully fueled, lifted itself, the second and third stages, and the spacecraft to a speed of 8,700 km (5,400 miles) per hour and to a point about 60 km (40 miles) above Earth.

The first stage was then jettisoned, and the second stage, powered by five smaller liquid-hydrogen-liquid-oxygen engines and weighing more than 450,000 kg (1,000,000 pounds), took over, increasing speed to more than 22,000 km (nearly 14,000 miles) per hour. At a point about 190 km (120 miles) above Earth, the second stage was jettisoned, and the liquid-fuel single-engine third stage ignited for about 2 ½ minutes to accelerate the spacecraft to 27,400 km (17,000 miles) per hour, putting it into a temporary parking orbit around Earth. The astronauts then reignited the third-stage engine, which burned for another 5 ½ minutes, cutting off at an altitude of about 300 km (190 miles) and a speed of about 40,000 km (25,000 miles) per hour, the velocity needed to escape Earth's gravity. Hours afterward the third stage was jettisoned while the spacecraft traveled on toward the Moon.

As director of the NASA George C. Marshall Space Flight Center in Huntsville, Ala., Wernher von Braun led the development of the large space launch vehicles, Saturn I, IB, and V. The engineering success of each of the Saturn class of space boosters, which contained millions of individual parts, remains unparalleled in rocket history. Each was launched successfully and on time and met safe performance requirements.

Moon rather than during the primordial heating event. Trace-element analyses indicate that the magmatic processes of partial melting gave rise to different lavas.

In addition to collecting samples, Apollo astronauts made geologic observations, took photographs, and placed long-lived instrument arrays and retro-reflectors on the lunar surface. Not only the landing expeditions but also the Apollo orbital observations yielded important new knowledge. On each mission the Moon-orbiting Command and Service modules carried cameras and remote-sensing instruments for gathering compositional information.

CHAPTER 4

THE SPACE SHUTTLE PROGRAM

After the success of the Apollo 11 mission, NASA proposed an ambitious plan that included human flights to Mars, a series of large space stations to be developed during the 1970s, and a new, reusable space transportation system to send people and supplies to those stations. This plan was quickly rejected, as there was no interest in major post-Apollo space programs among the political leadership or the general public.

In 1972 NASA received presidential approval to develop a partially reusable transport vehicle called a space shuttle. This vehicle was intended to carry people and as much as 29,500 kg (65,000 pounds) of cargo into low Earth orbit at low cost or, in other words, to be a "space truck." On the basis of those expectations, the United States planned to use the shuttle as its sole launch vehicle once it entered operation and to operate a shuttle fleet with a launch rate as high as 60 per year. In the absence of a space station, plans also called for having the shuttle serve double duty as a space platform to conduct in-orbit research for periods as long as two weeks. To that end, Europe pledged to contribute a pressurized laboratory, known as Spacelab, that would be carried in the shuttle's payload bay.

Formally called the Space Transportation System (STS), the U.S. space shuttle consists of three major components: a winged orbiter that carries both crew and cargo; an external tank containing liquid hydrogen (fuel) and liquid oxygen (oxidizer) for the orbiter's three main rocket engines; and a pair of large, solid-propellant, strap-on booster rockets. At liftoff the entire system weighs 2 million kilograms (4.4 million pounds) and stands 56 metres (184 feet) high. During launch the boosters and the orbiter's main engines fire together, producing about 31,000 kilonewtons (7 million pounds) of thrust. The boosters are jettisoned about two minutes after liftoff and are returned to Earth by parachute for reuse.

Eight minutes after liftoff, the orbiter has attained 99 percent of its orbital velocity and has exhausted the propellants in the external tank. It releases the tank, which disintegrates on reentering the atmosphere. Although the orbiter lifts off vertically like an expendable rocket launcher, it makes an unpowered descent and landing similar to a glider.

A fleet of four operational orbiters, named *Columbia*, *Challenger*, *Atlantis*, and *Discovery*, was built in order to allow multiple shuttle flights each year. Facilities in Florida originally constructed for the Apollo program were remodeled for shuttle use.

After several years of technical and budgetary delays to the program, the first space shuttle flight, STS-1. took place on April 12, 1981; aboard the *Columbia* orbiter were astronauts John W. Young, a veteran of the Gemini and Apollo programs, and Robert Laurel Crippen.

With additional shuttle flights, it became evident that projections of the vehicle's operational costs and performance (each shuttle had been expected to make 100 flights) had been extremely optimistic. Major refurbishment was required between each launch; the highest flight rate achieved was in 1985, when the shuttle was launched nine times. Each launch cost hundreds of millions of dollars, rather than the tens of millions that had been promised in 1972. Although the space shuttle was a remarkable technological achievement as a first-generation reusable launch vehicle, the plans to use it as the only launcher for American payloads proved to be a major policy mistake.

THE *CHALLENGER* DISASTER

Despite the miscalculation of its cost-effectiveness, the shuttle program was considered a qualified success from the payload standpoint. Missions to deploy satellites and conduct experiments in a low-gravity environment greatly advanced scientific research in biology, physics, and astronomy. The commercial applications of the shuttle program—delivering communications satellites for telecommunication companies, testing businesses' products in extreme conditions, ferrying personnel and equipment to build space stations—was considered promising during the first years of the program as well.

The primary goal of shuttle mission 51-L in 1986 was to launch a second Tracking and Data Relay Satellite (TDRS-B). It also carried the Spartan Halley spacecraft, a small satellite that was to be released by *Challenger* and picked up two days later after observing Halley's Comet during its closest approach to the Sun.

Christa McAuliffe. NASA/Johnson Space Center

Greatest visibility among the crew went to teacher-in-space Christa McAuliffe, of Concord, N.H., the winner of a national screening begun in 1984. McAuliffe was to conduct at least two lessons from orbit and then spend the following nine months lecturing to students across the United States. The goal was to highlight the importance of teachers and to interest students in high-tech careers. Other members of the crew were Francis (Dick) Scobee, pilot Michael Smith, mission specialists Ellison Onizuka, Judith Resnik, and Ronald McNair, and Hughes Aircraft engineer Gregory Jarvis.

The mission experienced trouble at the outset, as the launch was postponed for several days, partly because of delays in getting the previous shuttle mission, 61-C (*Columbia*), back on the ground. On the night before the launch, central Florida was swept by a severe cold wave that deposited thick ice on the launch pad. On launch day, January 28, liftoff was delayed until 11:38 AM.

All appeared to be normal until after the vehicle emerged from "Max-Q," the period of greatest aerodynamic pressure. Mission Control told Scobee, "*Challenger,* go with throttle up," and seconds later the vehicle disappeared in an explosion just 73 seconds after liftoff, at an altitude of 14,000 metres (46,000 feet). Tapes salvaged from the wreckage showed that the instant before breakup Smith said "Uh-oh," but nothing else was heard.

Debris rained into the Atlantic Ocean for more than an hour after the explosion. An intensive salvage operation was organized to retrieve as much of the wreckage as possible and the bodies of the crew. The task was complicated by the force of the explosion and the altitude at which it occurred, as well as the separate paths taken by the boosters. Searches revealed no sign of the crew.

DETERMINING A CAUSE

The incident immediately grounded the shuttle program. An intensive investigation by NASA and a commission appointed by U.S. Pres. Ronald Reagan and chaired by former secretary of state

William Rogers followed. Other members of the Rogers Commission included astronauts Neil Armstrong and Sally Ride, test pilot Chuck Yeager, and physicist Richard Feynman. What emerged was an appalling pattern of assumptions that the vehicle could survive minor mishaps and be pushed even further. The ill-fated launch brought to the fore the difficulties that NASA had been experiencing for many years in trying to accomplish too much with too little money.

The immediate cause of the accident was suspected within days and was fully established within a few weeks. The severe cold reduced the resiliency of two rubber O-rings that sealed the joint between the two lower segments of the right-hand solid rocket booster. (At a commission hearing, Feynman convincingly demonstrated the loss of O-ring resiliency by submerging an O-ring in a glass of ice water.) Under normal circumstances, when the shuttle's three main engines ignited they pressed the whole vehicle forward, and the boosters were ignited when the vehicle swung back to centre. On the morning of the accident, an effect called "joint rotation" occurred, which prevented the rings from resealing and opened a path for hot exhaust gas to escape from inside the booster. Puffs of black smoke appeared on the far side of the booster in a spot not visible to most cameras.

As the vehicle ascended, the leak expanded, and after 59 seconds a 2.4-metre (8-foot) stream of flame emerged from the hole. This grew to 12 metres (40 feet) and gradually eroded one of three struts that secured the booster's base to the large external fuel tank carrying liquid hydrogen and liquid oxygen for the orbiter engines. At the same time, thrust in the booster lagged slightly, although within limits, and the nozzle steering systems tried to compensate. When the strut broke, the booster's base swiveled outward, forcing its nose through the top of the external fuel tank and causing the whole tank to collapse and explode.

Through ground tracking cameras this was seen as a brief flame licking from a concealed spot on the right side of the vehicle a few seconds before everything disappeared in the explosion. Even if the plume had been seen at liftoff, there would have been no hope for crew escape, because the shuttle orbiter could not survive high-speed separation from the tank until the last seconds of the boosters' two-minute burn.

Challenger broke up in the explosion, but the forward section with the crew cabin was severed in one piece; it continued to coast upward with other debris, including wings and still-flaming engines, and then plummeted to the ocean. It was believed that the crew survived the initial breakup but that loss of cabin pressure rendered them unconscious within seconds since they did not wear pressure suits. Death probably resulted from oxygen deficiency minutes before impact.

The boosters also survived the fireball and righted themselves to continue flying, something totally unexpected. Range safety officers finally detonated their charges 30 seconds later to prevent them from overflying land. After the accident, NASA immediately began work on a redesigned solid booster for future launches.

The Rogers Commission report, delivered on June 6 to the president, faulted NASA as a whole, and its Marshall Space Flight Center in Huntsville, Ala., and contractor Morton Thiokol, Inc., in Ogden, Utah, in particular, for poor engineering and management. Marshall was responsible for the shuttle boosters, engines, and tank, while Morton Thiokol manufactured and assembled the booster motors at the Kennedy Space Center at Cape Canaveral, Fla.

The Rogers Commission heard disturbing testimony from a number of engineers who had been expressing concern about the reliability of the O-rings for at least two years and who had warned superiors about a possible failure the night before Challenger was launched. One of the Rogers Commission's strongest recommendations was to tighten the communication gap between shuttle managers and working engineers. In response to this implied criticism that its quality-control measures had become slack, NASA added several more checkpoints in the shuttle bureaucracy, including a new NASA safety office and a shuttle safety advisory panel, in order to prevent such a "flawed" decision to launch from being made again.

Aside from these internal fixes at NASA, however, the Rogers Commission also addressed a more fundamental problem. In NASA's efforts to streamline shuttle operations in pursuit of its declared goal of flying 24 missions a year, the commission said, the agency had simply been pushing too hard. The shuttle program had neither the personnel nor the spare parts to maintain such an ambitious flight rate without straining its physical resources or overworking its technicians.

AFTER *CHALLENGER*

This judgment cut to the core of the way in which the national space program had been conducted in the shuttle era. Indeed, the Challenger accident merely focused attention on more deeply seated problems that had existed for as long as 15 years. From the time it was approved by Pres. Richard Nixon in 1972, the shuttle had been conceived as a "do-everything" vehicle for carrying every kind of space payload, from commercial and scientific satellites to military spacecraft to probes bound for the outer planets. NASA's fleet of conventional "expendable" rockets such as the Delta and Atlas had been phased out in the shuttle era as a result and was being used primarily to reach polar orbits that the shuttle could not reach from Cape Canaveral.

Although this reliance on the shuttle was the officially stated national space policy, the Department of Defense began to retreat from relying exclusively on the shuttle even before the Challenger accident. Concerned that shuttle launch delays would jeopardize the assured access to space of high-priority national security satellites, the air force in 1985 began a program of buying advanced Titan rockets as "complementary expendable launch vehicles" for its own use.

Other, less powerful groups came forward after the *Challenger* accident to express their long-standing unhappiness with exclusive reliance on the shuttle for their access to space. Among those calling for a "mixed fleet" of shuttles and expendable launchers were scientists whose missions now faced long delays because the shuttle had become the only existing means of carrying their spacecraft.

By July, when NASA announced that the shuttle would not be ready to fly again until 1988, there was still no decision from Congress or the White House as to whether another orbiter would be built to replace *Challenger*. Proponents argued that another vehicle—perhaps two more—would be needed to meet the launch needs of the 1990s, which would include construction of NASA's international space station, a permanent facility in Earth orbit.

In mid-August, Pres. Ronald Reagan announced that construction of a replacement shuttle orbiter (later named *Endeavour*), would begin immediately. When the shuttle resumed service, however, it would no longer be in the business of launching commercial satellites for paying customers but would be devoted

Spacelab 1 module in the payload bay of the space shuttle orbiter Columbia *on the flight STS-9, which was launched on Nov. 28, 1983.* NASA

almost exclusively to defense and scientific payloads. The Reagan administration had long had the goal of stimulating a private space launch industry, and now, with the removal of a heavily subsidized

West German physicist-astronaut Ulf Merbold conducting a materials-processing experiment aboard Spacelab, carried into orbit in the payload bay of the space shuttle orbiter Columbia. NASA

competitor from the market, three different companies stepped forward within a week's time to announce plans for operating commercial versions of the Delta, Titan, and Atlas/Centaur launchers.

After the accident the shuttle fleet was grounded until September 1988. Upon the resumption of flights, the shuttle fleet was operated only with much greater assurances for the safety of its crew. This limited the flight rate to six to eight missions per year; the 100th shuttle flight was not achieved until October 2000.

SPACELAB

Both before and after the Challenger accident, the space shuttle demonstrated impressive capabilities in space operations, including the repair and redeployment of damaged satellites—most striking being the in-orbit repair of the Hubble Space Telescope in 1993. Moreover, the orbiter served as a space platform for conducting experiments and made observations of Earth and cosmic objects for as long as about two weeks.

On some missions the space shuttle carried in its payload bay a European-built pressurized facility called Spacelab, in which shuttle crew members have conducted biological and physical research in weightless conditions. The Spacelab facility had its origins at the same time as that of the shuttle program. In 1973 the European Space Research Organisation (which became the European Space Agency [ESA] in 1975) suggested it develop a "Research and Applications Module" as its principal contribution to space shuttle operations.

At that time NASA predicted the need for six modules. Europe was to fund the development and donate one module to NASA in return for an opportunity for its scientists to fly on the inaugural mission. The cost was to be recovered by producing the other five modules, which NASA would buy.

However, the shuttle failed to achieve the expected flight rate, and NASA bought the single module that it was obliged to accept and canceled its options for the others. (ESA had also built a second module for its own use.) The first flight was in 1983, with West German physicist Ulf Merbold as the European payload specialist. The cost of flying the shuttle proved so great that ESA eventually concluded that it could not afford to fund its own missions, so multinational missions were flown with U.S., Canadian, European, and Japanese programs sharing the cost.

Altogether, 25 flights were made with Spacelab for astronomical, solar, microgravity, life sciences, and materials sciences research. (Nine flights carried only unpressurized modules called pallets.) The advent of the International Space Station (ISS) rendered Spacelab obsolete, and the last flight of a pressurized module took place in April–May 1998. Pallets are still sometimes used to carry experiments to the ISS.

However, the shuttle has flown often enough that two U.S. astronauts, Franklin Chang-Díaz and Jerry Ross, have made seven spaceflights, the most by any single individual.

THE *COLUMBIA* DISASTER AND AFTER

In the first years of the 21st century, the space shuttle was flying several times a year. Many of these flights were dedicated to the construction of the ISS and carrying new crews and supplies there. Non-ISS shuttle flights were dedicated to important scientific projects, such as installing new instruments on the Hubble Space Telescope. However, the shuttle's record of success ended on Feb. 1, 2003, when the orbiter *Columbia* broke up on reentry, claiming the lives of all seven astronauts on board just minutes before it was to land at the Kennedy Space Center in Florida.

Columbia, which had made the shuttle program's first flight into space in 1981, lifted off for its 28th mission, STS-107, on Jan. 16, 2003. The flight was dedicated to various experiments that required a microgravity environment. The crew comprised commander Rick Husband; pilot William McCool; mission specialists Michael Anderson, David Brown, Kalpana Chawla, and Laurel Clark; and payload specialist Ilan Ramon, the first Israeli astronaut.

As *Columbia* was reentering Earth's atmosphere, it broke apart over Texas at approximately 9:00 AM Eastern Standard Time at an altitude of 60 km (40 miles), showering debris across southeastern Texas and southern Louisiana. The disintegration of the craft was recorded by television cameras and U.S. Air Force radar. Its major components and the remains of the crew were recovered over the following month.

The destruction of *Columbia* followed by almost exactly 17 years the loss of *Challenger* in a launch accident on Jan. 28, 1986. Ironically, the cause of the *Columbia* catastrophe soon was determined to be launch-related as well. Films showed that a piece of insulating foam broke loose from the external propellant tank and struck the leading edge of the left wing approximately 81 seconds after liftoff. Bits of foam had detached in past missions without serious mishap, and, at the time of the *Columbia* launch, NASA engineers did not think that the foam carried enough momentum to cause significant damage. In fact, as demonstrated in postaccident tests, the foam was capable of punching a large hole in the reinforced carbon-carbon insulation tiles that

Crew of the space shuttle Columbia (left to right)*: David Brown, Rick Husband, Laurel Clark, Kalpana Chawla, Michael Anderson, William McCool, and Ilan Ramon. The shuttle broke up catastrophically on Feb. 1, 2003, killing all aboard.* NASA

protected the shuttle's nose and wing leading edges from the extreme heat of atmospheric reentry. Although some engineers had wanted ground-based cameras to take photos of the orbiting shuttle to look for damage, the request did not get to the right officials.

During *Columbia*'s atmospheric reentry, hot gases penetrated the damaged tile section and melted major structural elements of the wing, which eventually collapsed. Data from the vehicle showed rising temperatures within sections of the left wing as early as 8:52 AM, although the crew knew of their situation for perhaps only a minute or so before vehicle breakup. Subsequent investigation by NASA and the independent Columbia Accident Investigation Board uncovered a number of managerial shortcomings, in addition to the immediate technical reason (poor manufacturing control of tank insulation and other defects), that allowed the accident to happen.

The most palpable result of the accident was a grounding of the remaining three shuttles—*Discovery*, *Atlantis*, and *Endeavour* (the last built to replace *Challenger*)—until NASA and its contractors could develop means to prevent similar accidents, which included kits for repairs in orbit.

CHAPTER 5

SPACE STATIONS

Through the years, elements of space exploration typically come to life in the vivid consciousness of human visionaries before they become a reality. For example, take the concept of space stations.

Before the first manned spaceflights, in a series of articles between 1952 and 1954 in the popular magazine *Collier's*, Wernher von Braun presented his vision of a space station as a massive wheel-shaped structure that would rotate to generate "artificial gravity" from centrifugal force, sparing its crew of 1,000 scientists and engineers the drawbacks of weightlessness. It would be serviced by a fleet of winged spaceships employing nuclear engines. One of the station's primary tasks would be to assemble vehicles for expeditions to the Moon.

That concept remained a popular portrait of humankind's future in space as late as 1968, when the American motion-picture director Stanley Kubrick's classic science-fiction film *2001: A Space Odyssey* depicted a spinning double-wheel station under construction above Earth. On a regular schedule, a fleet of commercial space planes flew people up to the station, from which they could catch a ferry to the Moon.

In Braun's day, the development of a space station was thought to be a preliminary stepping-stone to the Moon and planets, but, when Cold War politics prompted Pres. John F. Kennedy in 1961 to commit the United States to landing a man on the Moon before the decade was out, there was no time to pursue this logical route. Rather, a single spacecraft would be obliged to ride an expendable rocket into orbit and fly directly to its goal. Nevertheless, even as NASA plunged deeply into the Apollo program, it studied several space station strategies as part of an Apollo Applications Program, which would exploit vehicles built for the Moon race for more general orbital activities.

Even as *2001* was restating Braun's ambitious vision to the public, it already was obvious to space engineers that the first real space stations would have to be much simpler than their fictional counterparts. One NASA plan was to have an Apollo spacecraft dock with a spent rocket stage, whereupon its crew would pressurize the rocket's empty hydrogen-propellant tank with air and install scientific equipment that would turn it into a laboratory for several weeks of occupancy.

The U.S. Air Force had its own plan to operate a Manned Orbiting Laboratory fitted with an advanced camera to facilitate military reconnaissance activities. In 1969, however, just as NASA attained Kennedy's goal of a manned lunar landing, Pres. Richard M. Nixon canceled the Manned Orbiting Laboratory and restricted the Apollo Applications Program to a single station.

By 1969, even though the U.S.S.R. was still moving forward with its lunar landing program, it had begun to shift its emphasis in human spaceflight to the development of Earth-orbiting stations in which cosmonaut crews could carry out extended observations and experiments on missions that lasted weeks or months rather than a few days. Like the U.S. military, the Soviet Union had a plan to put a series of reconnaissance stations in orbit by the 1970s.

In 1969, with development running late for the large spacecraft that was to ferry crews and supplies to the station, Soviet officials decided to accelerate the program by employing the Soyuz spacecraft that had been developed during the failed attempt to win the Moon race. Moreover, because some of the systems needed for a military reconnaissance platform were not yet available, it was decided to initiate the program with a station equipped as a scientific laboratory.

SALYUT

The Soviet Union's space station design took the form of a stepped cylinder 14.6 metres (48 feet) long, with its widest section 4.25 metres (13.9 feet) in diameter. It was derived from the Almaz reconnaissance platform designed in the 1960s by Soviet aerospace engineer Vladimir Chelomey. Although the station could be oriented arbitrarily, its maneuvering engine was located immediately behind the wide section, which thus came to be defined as the rear of the station. At the front end was a docking system for Soyuz ferries. Internally, apart from an air lock in the cylindrical front section, the station formed a single rectangular room. The name of the station program, Salyut (Russian: "salute"), was chosen to honour cosmonaut Yury

Soyuz 10 before being positioned for launch at the Baikonur Cosmodrome in Kazakhstan. Carrying three cosmonauts, Soyuz 10 was launched April 23, 1971, to the Salyut 1 space station, which had been put into orbit four days earlier. Equipment malfunction prevented the cosmonauts from entering and occupying the station. Novosti Press Agency

Gagarin's historic first orbit of Earth a decade earlier.

Salyut 1, which was launched April 19, 1971, atop a Proton rocket, was outfitted from the start to support two three-man crews for a total of two months over a six-month period. Although its first designated crew docked five days later in Soyuz 10, the cosmonauts could not open their ferry's hatch and had to return home. Once the fault had been rectified, the crew of Soyuz 11—commander Georgy Dobrovolsky, test engineer Viktor Patsayev, and flight engineer Vladislav Volkov—spent 23 days aboard the station in June carrying out scientific studies, although tragedy struck on the way home when a valve in the descent capsule allowed the air to leak out, and the three

cosmonauts were killed. At that time, it was not Soviet practice for Soyuz cosmonauts to wear pressure suits.

In redesigning the Soyuz to prevent such an accident from recurring, one seat had to be omitted to accommodate a life-support system for two pressure-suited cosmonauts.

Launched in 1973, Salyut 2 suffered an explosion after being placed in orbit and was never occupied, but the U.S.S.R. managed a 16-day tour in July 1974 by the Soyuz 14 crew, commander Pavel Popovich and flight engineer Yury Artyukhin, aboard Salyut 3. This military reconnaissance variant resembled its predecessor but had its docking system at the rear rather than at the front.

The Soviet program achieved the operationally significant milestone of reoccupying a space station in 1975 when two crews lived aboard Salyut 4 for 30 and 63 days, respectively, and conducted scientific experiments. By the time Salyut 4 was abandoned, its environmental system had been exhausted, and the internal walls reportedly were laced with a smelly green mold. It served one final function, however, by receiving the prototype of an automated, unmanned form of the Soyuz spacecraft, called Progress, that was being developed to resupply future stations.

Salyut 5, occupied by two crews in 1976 and 1977 for 49 and 18 days, respectively, was another reconnaissance platform. Salyut 6, launched in September 1977, introduced the second generation of Soviet space stations. It had a docking

Soyuz T-5 spacecraft (foreground) *docked with the Salyut 7 space station, as photographed in orbit from Soyuz T-6. Salyut 7 was launched on April 19, 1982. Soyuz T-5, carrying the station's primary two-man crew, was launched nearly a month later, on May 13. Soyuz T-6, launched on June 24, carried three additional crew members, including a French guest cosmonaut, to the orbiting station.* Tass/Sovfoto

system at each end, which permitted Progress resupply ferries to link with an occupied station—i.e., while the crew's Soyuz was docked at the opposite end. The primary objective of this phase of the program was to extend crew endurance gradually in order to demonstrate that humans could survive in weightlessness for the length of time required for a round-trip journey to Mars, which was considered to be as long as 18 months.

STRETCHING THE LIMITS OF ENDURANCE

A major problem facing the endurance program was that the contemporary variant of the now-venerable Soyuz was limited to a two-month stay in space; beyond this time, its propellant system would deteriorate. This meant that, for a Salyut crew to remain aboard longer, its ferry would have to be replaced periodically. As a solution, endurance crews not only received Progress ferries but also hosted a succession of visitors (many from Soviet-allied countries) who would arrive in a fresh Soyuz, stay for a week or so, and then leave in the older Soyuz so that a usable crew-return craft was always available. By supporting crews for 684 days over a four-year period (with five long-duration crews unloading a dozen resupply craft and hosting 11 visiting crews), Salyut 6 greatly advanced the state of the art in space station operations.

One indicator of the rapid maturation of the Soviet program came when the two resident cosmonauts, commander Vladimir Lyakhov and flight engineer Valery Ryumin, made an impromptu space walk in August 1979 to cut away the frame of a radio telescope that had deployed incorrectly and blocked the rear docking port of the station.

A virtual copy of its predecessor, Salyut 7 was launched in April 1982. While extending the endurance record, a succession of crews were scheduled to occupy the station on a continuous basis, handing it over in an operational state. The cosmonauts' tours of duty would be more lonely because upgrades to the Soyuz—in its new guise it was called Soyuz T—allowed it to remain in space for six months, which obviated the need for frequent visitors.

On the other hand, life aboard would be more sociable because weight reduction had enabled the ferry's third seat to be reinstated. Most of the scientific apparatus to keep Salyut 7's crews busy was to be delivered in large modules that would dock temporarily with the station. Salyut 7 received two such modules— Cosmos 1443 in 1983 and Cosmos 1686 in 1985—on its front docking system.

Unfortunately, whereas Salyut 6 had had a run of exceptionally good luck, Salyut 7's very ambitious program was frustrated by a series of operational problems. Nevertheless, crews successfully undertook repairs of malfunctions so serious that, until they actually had been faced and overcome, they would have been considered cause to vacate the station. After a pipe of the space station's engine developed a propellant leak, specialized tools were fabricated and sent up, and members of the station's third main crew, commander Leonid Kizim and flight engineer Vladimir Solovyov, spacewalked in May 1984 to install a bypass.

Various setbacks had caused the first three crews to leave the station unattended. In February 1985, while temporarily vacant, Salyut 7 suffered a total power failure and started to drift. Four months later, after making a rendezvous without the assistance of the station's radar docking system, the fourth main crew, commander Vladimir Dzhanibekov and flight engineer Viktor Savinkyh, managed to link their Soyuz T-13 with the inert station and restore it to life. The objective of an in-space handover was not achieved until the Soyuz T-14 crew, comprising commander Vladimir Vasyutin, flight engineer Georgy Grechko, and research cosmonaut Aleksandr Volkov, arrived in September 1985, with the Soyuz T-13 cosmonauts still in residence. Salyut 7's bad luck continued to the end, when Vasyutin fell ill and the crew was recalled to Earth.

SKYLAB

The only element of NASA's Apollo Applications Program that did not succumb to Nixon's budgetary cuts was Skylab. Its plan, which called for a ready-to-use scientific laboratory that had been prefabricated on the ground, replaced the earlier concept of outfitting the tank of a spent rocket in space. Apollo spacecraft would ferry the crews and provide a very limited resupply capability.

Although similar in concept to Salyut in that its useful life was defined by its initial resources, Skylab was larger and much more capable because it used as its main habitat the third stage of the Saturn V vehicle that had launched the Apollo spacecraft to the Moon. The station's primary scientific instrument was the Apollo Telescope Mount (ATM), which at the time was by far the most powerful solar telescope ever placed in orbit. The ATM incorporated a number of component telescopes and other devices for observing the Sun over a broad range of the electromagnetic spectrum, from visible light through X-rays. Skylab also carried apparatus for Earth resources observations and materials science research.

On its launch on May 14, 1973, Skylab's thermal shielding was damaged, which made it necessary for the first crew to carry up and install an improvised "parasol" to allow the station to function at its planned level of operation. Over an eight-

U.S. Skylab space station in orbit over a cloud-covered Earth, photographed Feb. 8, 1974, by the departing third crew of astronauts from their Skylab 4 Command Module. The makeshift gold-coloured sun shield and underlying parasol on the main part of the station were installed by the first two crews to cover damage done to Skylab's protective shielding during launch. The launch mishap also tore off one of the station's lateral solar arrays. NASA

and-a-half-month period, Skylab hosted a trio of three-man crews for a total of nearly six months. Its final crew set an endurance record of almost three months; in the process, it undertook a detailed study of how the human body adapts to prolonged exposure to weightlessness—the Skylab program's most significant legacy.

Because of budget cuts, a planned second Skylab was never launched. Although plans called for Skylab to be used again by space shuttle crews, increased solar activity caused its orbit to degrade faster than expected. On July 11, 1979, it entered the atmosphere, broke up, and scattered debris over the southeastern Indian Ocean and Western Australia.

Salyut and Skylab were a reflection of a long-held belief among space visionaries, dating back to Tsiolkovsky at the start of the 20th century, that living and working in space, first in Earth orbit and then on the Moon, Mars, and other locations, were an important part of the human future. It also was thought that increasingly complex orbital outposts would be the first steps in a long-term process of space development and colonization. The early focus of the United States and the U.S.S.R. on sending people to the Moon for political reasons deviated from this vision, which has since returned to dominate space thinking.

MIR

Soviet officials decided to scrap the jinxed Salyut 7 and advance to the next phase, which was to assemble a large modular complex in orbit. At its core would be a base block derived from the Salyut design, which would be outfitted as the crew habitat. The base block had the form of a stepped cylinder about 13 metres (43 feet) long and 4.2 metres (13.8 feet) in diameter at its widest point. In addition to a pair of axial docking systems, it would have a ring of four peripheral docking units around its nose to accept modules mounted at right angles to the base block. Five add-on units would expand the station and provide its primary scientific instruments. To mark the advance, the new station was called Mir (Russian: "peace," "community," or "world.")

Mir's base block was launched on Feb. 20, 1986, and was placed into the same orbital plane as Salyut 7. This allowed Mir's commissioning crew, commander Leonid Kizim and Vladimir Solovyov, to shuttle between the two stations in their Soyuz T in order to wrap up Salyut 7's program and salvage usable apparatus from the older station. Like Salyut 7, Mir was intended to be occupied on a continuous basis, but delays in building the first of the add-on modules led to the station's being vacated for a time. When the second crew, commander Yury Romanenko and flight engineer Aleksandr Laveykin, set off for Mir in February 1987, it was in a new form of Soyuz, called Soyuz TM.

In April the cosmonauts received the first of the expansion modules, Kvant 1. Mounted at the rear of the Mir base block, Kvant 1 was primarily an astrophysical observatory, but it also provided systems for attitude control and life support and carried a docking system at the rear for ferries. The second add-on, Kvant 2, was launched in November 1989 and carried additional life-support systems and a large air lock. It was first docked axially at the front of the station and then swung around to a perpendicular position by a mechanical arm, an adjustment that made the station L-shaped.

In May 1990 docking of the third module, Kristall, a materials-processing factory, transformed the L configuration into a T. Spektr (launched May 1995) and Priroda (launched April 1996), two science modules containing remote-sensing instruments for ecological and environmental studies of Earth, completed the station. With the exception of its first occupants, Mir's cosmonaut crews traveled between the station and Earth in upgraded Soyuz TM spacecraft, and supplies were transported by robotic Progress cargo ferries.

Beginning in September 1989, Mir was continuously inhabited for nearly a decade by a succession of crews. Although in most cases they served a standard six-month tour of duty, Valery Polyakov, a physician, spent a record 14 months aboard in 1994–95, longer than the approximately nine months estimated for a manned voyage to the planet Mars.

It had been hoped to complete Mir within three years, use it for several years, and then start assembly of its successor by utilizing the Soviet version of the U.S. space shuttle, called *Buran*, then under development. By the time Kristall was added in mid-1990, however, the base block already was approaching its five-year design life. Delays in developing *Buran* meant that Mir's service life would have to be extended.

In 1991, on the demise of the Soviet Union, *Buran* was canceled and funding for Mir reduced. Facing a financial crisis, the newly created Russian Space Agency offered Mir to the international community as a microgravity research laboratory, selling time aboard it for a fee. In the early 1990s, several of Europe's space agencies accepted the offer and sent astronauts to Mir to conduct a variety of microgravity studies.

Designed for only a five-year life, the aging Mir suffered a series of equipment failures and accidents in 1996–97, in the midst of the joint U.S.-Russia Shuttle-Mir program. The most spectacular of these were a fire in the Kvant 1 module on Feb. 24, 1997, and a collision of a Progress ship with the Spektr module on June 25, 1997, that briefly depressurized the space station.

Nevertheless, Mir remained in service until June 15, 2000, when the last crew, commander Sergey Zalyotin and flight engineer Aleksandr Kaleri, departed. Mir supported human habitation from 1986

U.S. space shuttle Atlantis *docked with the Russian space station* Mir, *in a photograph taken by cosmonaut Nikolay Budarin from a Russian Soyuz spacecraft on July 4, 1995.* NASA

to 2000, which included an uninterrupted stretch of occupancy of almost 10 years, and hosted 100 people from 12 countries. On March 23, 2001, the abandoned Mir made a controlled reentry, with the surviving pieces falling into the Pacific Ocean.

THE INTERNATIONAL SPACE STATION

In 1969, NASA proposed to President Nixon that a reusable space shuttle be developed to serve as the basis for post-Apollo activities in Earth orbit. At that time, still pursuing Braun's vision of a space plane and complementary orbiting base, the agency had hoped to use the shuttle to build a space station, but the high cost of funding the first project precluded starting the second. Once the shuttle was in service, however, the agency again began lobbying for a station. In 1984, Pres. Ronald Reagan ordered that a space station be developed within a decade and that it involve international participation. Unfortunately, because of legislative disputes over the station's design and cost and various setbacks to NASA's overall space program, no actual construction was begun during the assigned period.

In 1993, as the prospect of cancellation loomed, Pres. Bill Clinton ordered NASA to widen the multinational partnership by including Russia, with which relations had dramatically improved following the end of the Cold War. In an extension of that spirit of cooperation, the United States and Russia agreed to merge their respective space station developments into a program for a single orbital structure, the International Space Station (ISS).

The first phase of the integrated program called for a series of shuttle missions to Mir to allow NASA to gain practical experience operating in conjunction with a station and to make an early start on microgravity research. On June 29, 1995, the space shuttle *Atlantis* docked with Mir, which was the first time astronauts and cosmonauts had met in space since the Apollo-Soyuz Test Project 20 years earlier. Seven American astronauts eventually spent months on Mir.

NASA's interest in Mir was strictly as a stepping-stone, and it intended soon after the final shuttle-Mir mission in early 1998 to put into orbit the first element of the ISS. Launched by Russia atop a Proton rocket in late 1998, the initial module, called Zarya, was designed to provide attitude control and solar power arrays for the nascent station. Shortly afterward, space shuttle astronauts ferried up and attached the first U.S.-built element, named Unity, a connecting node with multiple docking systems.

Development difficulties delayed the launch of the next ISS element, Zvezda, a crew habitat and control centre similar to the Mir base block, until mid-2000. Two weeks after it was carried up on a Proton rocket, Zvezda rendezvoused and docked automatically at the trailing end of Zarya. Later in the year, the first resident ISS crew, comprising two Russians, flight engineers Yury Gidzenko and Sergey Krikalyov, and

Crews from three countries having a meal in the Zvezda module of the International Space Station, 2001. NASA

an American, commander William Shepherd, arrived in Soyuz TM-31.

Subsequent installation of a large solar power array and cooling radiators on a truss mounted on Unity cleared the way for the shuttle launch of NASA's microgravity laboratory, Destiny, in early 2001. The addition of Destiny, which astronauts mated to the leading end of Unity, marked a milestone in the project because it facilitated science operations.

Aside from the United States and Russia, station construction involved Canada, Japan, Brazil, and 11 ESA members. Russian modules were carried into space by Russian expendable launch vehicles, after which they automatically rendezvoused with and docked to the ISS. Other elements were ferried up by space shuttle and assembled in orbit during space walks.

Both shuttles and Russian Soyuz spacecraft transported people to and from the station. The Soyuz TMA debuted in 2002 with a manned flight to the ISS; its design incorporated changes to meet NASA requirements as an ISS "lifeboat," including eased height and weight restrictions for crew members. An upgraded version of Progress was also used to ferry cargo to the ISS.

Much of the early research work by ISS astronauts was to focus on long-term life-sciences and material-sciences

The International Space Station photographed against the Rio Negro, Argentina, from the shuttle orbiter Atlantis, *Feb. 16, 2001.* Atlantis's *primary mission was to deliver the Destiny laboratory module, visible at the leading end of the station.* NASA

investigations in the weightless environment. After the breakup of the space shuttle orbiter *Columbia* in February 2003, the shuttle fleet was grounded, which effectively halted expansion of the station. Meanwhile, the crew was reduced from three to two, and their role was restricted mainly to caretaker status, limiting the amount of science that could be done. Crews flew up to and returned from the ISS in Soyuz spacecraft, and the station was serviced by automated Progress ferries. After the shuttle resumed regular flights in 2006, the ISS crew size was increased to three.

Construction resumed in September of that year, with the addition of a pair of solar wings and a thermal radiator. The European-built American node, Harmony, was placed on the end of Destiny in October 2007. Harmony has a docking port for the space shuttle and connecting ports for a European laboratory, Columbus, and a Japanese laboratory, Kibo. In February 2008 Columbus was mounted on Harmony's starboard side. Columbus was Europe's first long-duration manned space laboratory and contained experiments in such fields as biology and fluid dynamics. In the following month, an improved variant of the Ariane V rocket

U.S. astronaut Peggy Whitson (right), Expedition 16 commander, greeting astronaut Pam Melroy, STS-120 commander, after the opening of the hatch between the International Space Station and the space shuttle Discovery, Oct. 25, 2007. NASA

launched Europe's heaviest spacecraft, the Jules Verne Automated Transfer Vehicle (ATV), which carried 7,700 kg (17,000 pounds) of supplies to the ISS. Also in March 2008 shuttle astronauts brought the Canadian robot, Dextre, which was so sophisticated that it would be able to perform tasks that previously would have required astronauts to make space walks, and the first part of Kibo. In June 2008 the main part of Kibo was installed. An external platform was attached to the far end of Kibo in 2009.

Also in 2009, the ISS began hosting a six-person crew, which will require two Soyuz lifeboats to be docked with the ISS at all times. In 2010, a third node will be installed, and mounted on this will be a cupola, whose robotic work station and many windows will better enable astronauts to supervise external operations.

After the completion of the ISS, the shuttle will be retired from service. Thereafter the ISS will be serviced by Russia's Progress, Europe's ATV, and a variety of commercial cargo vehicles that are currently under development in the United States. Until NASA's Orion spacecraft launches in 2015, astronauts will use Soyuz spacecraft to reach the ISS.

CHAPTER 6

FUTURE DIRECTIONS

The future of space exploration will undoubtedly be determined in large part by emerging developments in manned spaceflight. In the United States, the space shuttle program, which is scheduled to be permanently grounded as of 2010, will be replaced by craft that is designed to meet and exceed the shuttles' capabilities. Refinements to first-generation orbital craft such as the Apollo rockets are expected to usher in a new era in space travel. Scientists predict the world should soon see advances in space exploration that will not only take humans back to the Moon, but propel them forward to prospective colonies on Mars and other new frontiers within our galaxy.

CONSTELLATION PROGRAM

In January 2004 Pres. George W. Bush called upon NASA to resume manned missions to the Moon and then to begin manned missions to Mars. A key requirement was that this new program be funded by retiring the space shuttle in 2010 after completing the ISS. Although under review as of Summer 2009, the successor to the space shuttle program should be the Constellation program. Its earliest flights are planned to carry astronauts to the International Space Station (ISS) beginning in 2015. However, missions to the Moon by 2020 and to Mars after that are the main focus of Constellation.

The new program, named after the U.S. Navy's first ship, comprises launch vehicles, a manned spacecraft, and a lunar

Artist's conception of the Orion manned spacecraft orbiting the Moon. NASA/Lockheed Martin Corp.

lander. A number of lift options were considered for the Constellation program, including the use of existing Delta IV and the Atlas V launchers. However, it was ultimately decided to modify proven space shuttle components—in particular, the space shuttle main engine (SSME), the solid rocket booster (SRB), and the external tank (ET)—in order to create new vehicles.

In June 2006 NASA named the new launchers Ares, after the Greek counterpart of the Roman god Mars. Ares I is designed to carry the manned spacecraft, and the larger Ares V is designed to carry heavier cargo like the lunar lander. The Roman numerals assigned to the launchers are a tribute to the Saturn vehicles of the Apollo program.

The two-stage Ares I will launch the Orion spacecraft with either six astronauts to the International Space Station (ISS) or four to the Moon. Its first stage will be a five-segment SRB based on the shuttle's four-segment version. An upper stage will be powered by a modernized version of the J-2 hydrogen-burning engine developed for the upper stages of the Saturn launch vehicles. On top of this upper stage will be the Orion spacecraft, which will have an escape tower on its

apex. These components give the 97.8-metre- (321-foot-) tall Ares I its distinctive profile, earning it the nickname "the stick." The first stage of Ares I will be recoverable (as is the case with the space shuttle's SRBs), but the upper stage will be expendable. Ares I will be able to deliver a payload of some 25,000 kg (55,000 pounds) to low Earth orbit.

The first Ares I test vehicle comprised a surplus shuttle SRB fitted with an inert fifth segment, a nonfunctional upper stage, and a model of Orion outfitted with instrumentation to report on conditions in flight. A second test vehicle will use a functional upper stage and spacecraft. The first launch with a crew is scheduled for 2015; the spacecraft will visit the ISS. Lunar missions are planned to occur by 2020 and missions to Mars as soon as practicable thereafter.

Ares V initially will launch the Altair lunar lander but later will deliver to low Earth orbit the components of the large vehicle that will fly to Mars. It will be 110 metres (358 feet) tall and will have a pair of SRBs similar to that of the Ares I and strapped to a core stage that will consist of an enlarged ET with a cluster of six RS-68 engines at its base. These engines were developed for the Delta IV and have a sea-level thrust of 2,890,000 newtons (650,000 pounds) each. The second stage will be powered by the same engine as the Ares I upper stage. The payload to low Earth orbit will be 130,000 kg (287,000 pounds).

In August 2006, the manned space-craft, initially dubbed the Crew Exploration Vehicle, was named Orion after the constellation. Orion is 5 metres (16 feet) in diameter and has a launch mass of 22,700 kilograms (50,000 pounds). It consists of a conical crew module and a cylindrical service module, and it will be able to spend six months docked to the ISS. The crew module has a volume of 20 cubic metres (700 cubic feet), half of which will be habitable. It will be able to carry a crew of six to the ISS or four on a lunar mission.

The service module will house the main propulsion system, the attitude control system, and oxygen and water for the crew module. The overall configuration is reminiscent of the Apollo spacecraft, but the service module will draw power from deployable solar panels rather than from fuel cells. A prototype Orion was delivered to NASA in late 2007. The first test launch will be in 2009, and the first launch with a crew is scheduled to be directed to the ISS in 2015.

In December 2007, NASA named the lunar lander Altair, after the brightest star in the constellation Aquila. Aquila is the Latin word for eagle, which was also the name of the first manned spacecraft to land on the Moon, Apollo 11's lunar module.

Altair will be a two-stage spacecraft (a descent stage and an ascent stage) and will land four astronauts on the Moon. Its launch mass will be 37,800 kilograms (83,300 pounds). For a manned mission to

Artist's conception of the Ares V cargo launch vehicle shortly after liftoff. NASA/MSFC

Artist's conception of a possible design for the Altair lunar lander. NASA

the Moon, an Ares V will be launched first, carrying Altair into Earth's orbit. An Ares I will then launch with Orion, which will dock with Altair's ascent stage. The second stage of the Ares V will reignite to send Altair and Orion to the Moon, after which the docked spacecraft will withdraw from the spent stage. The service module's main engine will slow Altair and Orion so they can enter lunar orbit. The crew of four will transfer to Altair and land on the Moon. On the early missions the surface expedition will last a week.

The descent stage of Altair will serve as a launch platform for the ascent stage, which will rendezvous in lunar orbit with Orion. The crew will then transfer to Orion, after which the ascent stage will be jettisoned. The service module's main engine will be used to leave lunar orbit. Just before the spacecraft reenters Earth's atmosphere, the service module will be jettisoned. The capsule will then discard its basal heat shield and deploy its three parachutes. The normal mode of return will be on land in the United States, but if necessary the capsule will be able to splash down at sea.

EMERGING SPACE PROGRAMS

Space programs other than those run by the United States and Russia have steadily made progress over the course of the late 20th and early 21st century. Of special note, particularly with regard to manned spaceflight, is the Chinese program, which

HUMAN EXPLORATION OF MARS

The ultimate goal of the Constellation program is to establish a research base on Mars. Human exploration of that planet is still decades away despite optimism when the Apollo program ended in the early 1970s that Mars exploration would soon follow. The technical difficulties of getting people to Mars and back, while challenging, are not overwhelming. The main difficulty has been in coming up with a compelling rationale that would justify the tremendous costs and risks. Advocates have argued that exploring Mars and extending human reach beyond Earth-Moon space needs no practical rationale; to explore is an essential part of being human. Others have argued that practical benefits such as economic stimulus, scientific discovery, and technology feedback would result.

Several studies have been undertaken to determine how human missions to Mars might be implemented. There are two basic classes of missions that follow from the orbital motions of Mars and Earth. In opposition-class missions, the round-trip time is 500–600 days, with 30 days spent on Mars. For conjunction-class missions, the round-trip time is about 900 days, and the time spent on Mars may be as much as 550 days. Most studies conclude that the short stay time for opposition-class missions could not justify the cost and effort of getting there and that, despite the greater resources needed, a conjunction-class mission is preferred.

There are many variants on how such a mission might be implemented. In some scenarios a cargo ship is sent ahead of the humans to establish a robotically operated base, and the humans follow, possibly years later. In other variants all the resources needed accompany the crew. Another issue is the extent to which resources at Mars could be used for supporting people during their stay and for making oxidants and propellants for the return trip. In situ resource units (ISRUs) could be sent to Mars well ahead of the people to extract and store both oxygen from the atmosphere and hydrogen from water, using solar or nuclear power. People would not be launched from Earth until adequate resources for mission success had accumulated at Mars.

To save fuel, the atmosphere at both Mars and Earth could be used to decelerate (aerobrake) the outgoing and incoming spacecraft, respectively; an additional option is direct entry. Another issue is what the astronauts would do at Mars. Should they stay close to a base and operate remote robots at various locations around the planet, or should they go on extended trips from the base and explore, thereby incurring the risk of being stranded?

One issue that is not so readily susceptible to quantitative engineering analysis is crew health. Long times in space have various physiological effects. The circulatory and vestibular systems are affected, and bones tend to demineralize. Countermeasures to minimize degradation in human performance would have to be devised. The crew would also experience psychological pressures from several hundred days in a confined space far from Earth with no other company. Radiation effects would also be significant, particularly if solar storms occurred during the two–three year trip.

Planetary protection is another issue. The first concern is scientific: Mars should not be contaminated with terrestrial materials before the potential for indigenous life has been adequately assessed. Robotic spacecraft sent to Mars are subject to rigorous cleanliness requirements, and parts that touch the surface are sterilized to minimize the possibility of interfering with the detection of indigenous life. Clearly, similar protective measures cannot be followed for human missions.

The second issue concerns back contamination. International protocols require that materials returned from Mars be quarantined until they have been proved to be safe. The astronauts may similarly have to be quarantined. Fortunately, most of the planetary-protection issues should be resolvable well ahead of human missions by robotic return of Martian samples.

sent humans into orbit in 2003 during the first Shenzhou mission.

The Chinese Shenzhou (Chinese for "divine craft") spacecraft is similar in design to the Russian Soyuz spacecraft. Like Soyuz, Shenzhou consists of three modules: a cylindrical rear module that contains instrumentation and the propulsion system, a bell-shaped middle module that carries the crew during launch and landing, and a cylindrical forward orbital module that carries scientific and military experiments. Unlike the Soyuz, the orbital module is capable of independent flight. On several Shenzhou missions, the orbital module remained in orbit for several months after its separation from the reentry module.

Shenzhou is 9.3 metres (30.5 feet) long and weighs 7,840 kg (17,280 pounds). The launch vehicle is a Chang Zheng 2F (CZ-2F, or Long March 2F), a version of the CZ-2 specifically developed for the Shenzhou program.

In 1997, China selected 12 military test pilots, all men, for its first group of trainee taikonauts—the Chinese term for astronaut. The first four Shenzhou missions were unmanned test flights launched over a three-year period (1999–2002). On Oct. 15, 2003, Shenzhou 5 carried the first Chinese astronaut, pilot Yang Liwei, on a 21-hour spaceflight. China thus became the third country after Russia and the United States to launch a manned spacecraft.

Shenzhou 6 was launched on Oct. 12, 2005, lasted five days, and carried two astronauts. Shenzhou 7 was launched on Sept. 25, 2008, and carried three astronauts; one of them, commander Zhai Zhigang, made the first Chinese space walk. Future plans for the Shenzhou program include complex rendezvous maneuvers and the assembly of a space station from Shenzhou 8 and a laboratory module, Tiangong 1.

SPACE TOURISM

Since its inception, manned spaceflight has been mainly the purview of a select few individuals—specially trained professional aircraft pilots, scientists, medical personnel, and engineers. Intense training is still required of anyone participating in orbital and suborbital flight. But the list of those who now travel into space has expanded to include wealthy adventurers. Both government programs and private companies have made inroads on the quest to make outer space a travel destination.

A spirit of international cooperation is what made "recreational" spaceflight, commonly referred to as space tourism, possible. The advent of space tourism occurred at the end of the 1990s with a deal between the Russian company MirCorp and the American company Space Adventures, Ltd. MirCorp was a private venture in charge of the space station Mir. To generate income for maintenance of the aging space station, MirCorp decided to sell a trip to Mir. American businessman Dennis Tito became its first paying passenger. However, before Tito could make his trip, the decision was made to deorbit Mir. After the intervention of Space Adventures, Ltd., the mission was diverted to the ISS. Five of the first six space tourists have been American.

DENNIS TITO (b. Aug. 8, 1940, Queens, N.Y., U.S.)

American businessman Dennis Tito was the first private individual to pay for his own trip into space. Tito earned a B.S. in astronautics and aeronautics from New York University in 1962 and an M.S. in engineering science from Rensselaer Polytechnic Institute in Troy, N.Y., in 1964. He worked as an aerospace engineer in NASA's Jet Propulsion Laboratory, where he helped to plan and monitor the Mariner 4 and 9 missions to Mars.

In 1972 he moved from astronautics to finance when he helped found the American investment firm Wilshire Associates and created the Dow Jones Wilshire 5000 Composite Index, a measure of U.S. securities markets. He is credited with having innovated the now-established use of mathematical tools, borrowed from his work in astronautics, to determine financial market risks.

Throughout the 1990s Tito negotiated with space agencies in Moscow before securing passage on a 2001 mission to the space station Mir at the cost of $20 million. He began training in 2000 at the Yury Gagarin Cosmonaut Training Centre in Star City, Russia, but the mission was canceled when Russia allowed the Mir station to crash to Earth. Instead, on April 28, 2001, Tito joined two Russian cosmonauts, commander Talgat Musabayev and flight engineer Yury Baturin, on a supply mission, Soyuz TM-32, to the International Space Station (ISS). The move caused some controversy at NASA, which felt that Tito needed several weeks of training at NASA facilities before going to the ISS. Tito stayed six days aboard the ISS before returning aboard Soyuz TM-31. Tito and the Soyuz crew parachuted to Earth on May 6, landing in the steppes of Kazakhstan.

Given the arduous training required for his mission, Tito objected to the use of the term space tourist, and since his flight the term spaceflight participant has been more often used to distinguish space travelers from career astronauts. After his historic flight, Tito returned to his position at Wilshire Associates.

GREGORY OLSEN (b. April 20, 1945, Brooklyn, N.Y., U.S.)

American scientist and entrepreneur Gregory Hammond Olsen was the third space tourist. Olsen earned a bachelor of science degree in physics in 1966, a bachelor of science degree in electrical engineering in 1968, and a master of science degree in physics in 1968 from Fairleigh Dickinson University in Madison, N.J. He later received a doctorate in materials science from the University of Virginia at Charlottesville in 1971 and did postdoctoral research at the University of Port Elizabeth in South Africa from 1971 to 1972.

Between 1972 and 1983 Olsen taught physics and worked as a research scientist at RCA Laboratories in Princeton, N.J. He cofounded his first company, EPITAXX, Inc., a manufacturer of fibre-optic detectors, in 1984. After selling EPITAXX for $12 million in 1990, Olsen cofounded Sensors Unlimited, Inc., a manufacturer of near-infrared cameras and a developer of optoelectronic devices for fibre-optic communications systems, in 1992. Olsen served as the chief executive officer, and the company was sold for approximately $700 million in 2000 (and later repurchased and resold by Olsen's management team).

Olsen's participation in the Russian space program was organized by Space Adventures, Ltd., an American space tourism company. Although the ticket price was not publicly disclosed, it is estimated that Olsen paid approximately $20 million for the trip under a commercial agreement with the Russian Federal Space Agency. After receiving five months of cosmonaut training at the Yury Gagarin Cosmonaut Training Centre in Star City, Russia, Olsen launched into space on Oct. 1, 2005, aboard Soyuz TMA-7 with commander Valery Tokarev of Russia and flight engineer William McArthur of the United States. Soyuz TMA-7 docked with the International Space Station (ISS) on Oct. 3, 2005.

Olsen assisted the crew in conducting various life science experiments on the ISS, including an examination of the effect of microgravity on cell surfaces and intercellular interactions and an investigation of the effects of radiation exposure on human organs. Olsen also carried out several self-designed experiments in remote sensing and astronomy and tested equipment for his firm, Sensors Unlimited, while in space. He returned to Earth aboard Soyuz TMA-6 on October 11.

After his 10-day trip in space, Olsen returned to his entrepreneurial activities, founding GHO Ventures, LLC, where he served as president and managed his various investments in business ventures.

Anousheh Ansari (b. Sept. 12, 1966, Meshed, Iran)

Iranian-born American businesswoman Anousheh Ansari was the first female space tourist, the first person of Iranian descent, and the first Muslim woman to go into space. Ansari emigrated from Iran to the United States in 1984 as a teenager. She earned a bachelor's degree in electronics and computer engineering from George Mason University, Fairfax, Va., in 1988 and a master's degree in electrical engineering from George Washington University, Washington, D.C., while working full-time at MCI Communications.

In 1993, Ansari, her husband, Hamid Ansari, and her brother-in-law, Amir Ansari, cofounded Telecom Technologies, Inc. The company was acquired by Sonus Networks, Inc., in 2000 in a deal worth approximately $550 million.

Ansari's interest in space exploration was in evidence before her spaceflight. In 2002, Ansari and her brother-in-law made a multimillion-dollar contribution to the X Prize Foundation, a non-profit organization that manages competitions to encourage innovations that benefit humanity. The Ansari family's gift was used to fund the Ansari X Prize, a cash award of $10 million for the first private company to launch a reusable manned spacecraft into space twice within two weeks. In 2004 the aerospace development company Scaled Composites of Mojave, Calif., won the Ansari X Prize with SpaceShipOne, a vehicle conceived by American aircraft designer Burt Rutan.

Ansari arranged to participate in a spaceflight through Space Adventures, Ltd. Although the exact terms of the deal remained private, Ansari was estimated to have paid around $20 million for her participation in the mission. In early 2006 she began spaceflight training in Star City, Russia, originally as a backup for Enomoto Daisuke, a Japanese businessman. When Enomoto was disqualified from flying on the mission for medical reasons, Ansari replaced him on the flight crew of Soyuz TMA-9.

Ansari lifted off into space on Sept. 18, 2006, with commander Mikhail Tyurin of Russia and flight engineer Michael Lopez-Alegria of the United States. On Sept. 20, 2006, the spacecraft docked to the

International Space Station, where Ansari spent eight days. She performed a series of experiments concerning human physiology for the European Space Agency, was interviewed from space for an astronomy show on Iranian national television, and published dispatches and answered questions on her blog while stationed on the ISS (thereby becoming the first person to blog from space). She returned to Earth aboard Soyuz TMA-8, landing in Kazakhstan on Sept. 29, 2006.

After completing her space mission, Ansari continued to work as a businesswoman and entrepreneur. In 2006 she cofounded Prodea Systems, a digital technology company, and served as the company's first chief executive officer. Prodea announced a partnership with Space Adventures, Ltd., and the Federal Space Agency of Russia to create a fleet of suborbital spacecraft for commercial use.

CHARLES SIMONYI (b. Sept. 10, 1948, Budapest, Hung.)

Hungarian-born American software executive Charles Simonyi was the first repeat space tourist. Simonyi (born Simonyi Karolyi) left Hungary in 1966 to work at the Danish computer company Regnecentralen. He graduated from the University of California, Berkeley, with a degree in engineering mathematics and later earned a doctorate in computer science from Stanford University.

After working at the Xerox Palo Alto Research Center (Xerox PARC)—where he created the first WYSIWYG (what you see is what you get) text editor—from 1972 to 1980, Simonyi joined the Microsoft Corporation in 1981. While at Microsoft he led the development of the widely used software applications Microsoft Word and Microsoft Excel. In 2002 he left Microsoft to found his own firm, Intentional Software. In 2007, for the price of $20 million, he became the fifth paying traveler sent into space by Space Adventures, Ltd.

After a six-month training program at the Yury Gagarin Cosmonaut Training Centre in Star City, Russia, Simonyi launched into space from the Baikonur Cosmodrome in Kazakhstan aboard Soyuz TMA-10 on April 7, 2007, with two Russian cosmonauts, Expedition 15 commander Fyodor Yurchikhin and flight engineer Oleg Kotov. On April 9 he arrived at the International Space Station (ISS), where he spent 11 days performing scientific experiments and communicating via amateur radio with high school students. He returned to Earth aboard Soyuz TMA-9, landing in the Kazakhstan steppes on April 21.

In 2008 he bought a seat for a second flight to the ISS. On March 26, 2009, he lifted off with Russian cosmonaut Gennady Padalka and U.S. astronaut Michael Barratt aboard Soyuz TMA-14, a flight to the ISS that made Simonyi the first repeat space tourist. He returned to Earth aboard Soyuz TMA-13 on April 8.

RICHARD GARRIOTT (b. July 4, 1961, Cambridge, Eng.)

British-born American computer-game developer Richard Allen Garriott was the sixth space tourist and the first second-generation American to go into space. Garriott grew up in Houston the son of NASA astronaut Owen Garriott, who first flew into space on July 28, 1973, as part of the Skylab 3 mission. Many of the Garriotts' friends and neighbours were astronauts, and Garriott developed an early interest in spaceflight.

While Garriott never abandoned his dreams of spaceflight, his interests and career path took him into the computer-gaming industry. In the 1980s, while attending the University of Texas at Austin, he developed his first video game, Ultima 1. The Ultima series that followed established him as a major player in the computer-gaming industry, and in 1983 Garriott cofounded Origin Systems, Inc. In 1997 Garriott and his team created Ultima Online, a pioneer in the burgeoning genre of online computer games. Three years later he started Destination Games, which later became part of NCsoft, the world's largest online-game developer and publisher. In November 2007 he launched the multiplayer online computer game Tabula Rasa.

Garriott became the fifth American space tourist, and the sixth overall, when, after training at the Yury Gagarin Cosmonaut Training Centre in Star City, Russia, he launched aboard Soyuz TMA-13 on Oct. 12, 2008, with commander Yury Lonchakov of Russia and flight engineer Edward Fincke of the United States. He arrived at the International Space Station (ISS) two days later.

Garriott's work on the ISS included communicating with students via radio signals, taking photographs for the Nature Conservancy, and conducting experiments on the physiological effects of space travel. He landed in Kazakhstan aboard Soyuz TM-12 on Oct. 23, 2008. His trip was made possible by Space Adventures, Ltd., in which Garriott was an investor.

SpaceShipOne

Although the orbital space tourism industry garnered much media attention following Tito's flight, other companies were also hard at work trying to make space tourism a profitable proposition by developing suborbital vehicles designed to take passengers to an altitude of 100 km (62 miles). Since 2007, Space Adventures has offered a spaceflight around the Moon on a Soyuz spacecraft for a fee of $100 million.

With financing from Microsoft cofounder Paul Allen, SpaceShipOne (SS1) was designed and developed by Scaled Composites of Mojave, Calif., an aerospace development company founded by American aircraft designer Burt Rutan in 1982. The space vehicle was part of a broader program known as Tier One, which was made up of SS1, a launch aircraft called White Knight (WK), a hybrid rocket engine system using rubber and liquid nitrous oxide as the fuels, and an avionics suite. Scaled Composites had previously developed dozens of unique composite material aircraft.

To launch SS1 directly from the ground would have required a great deal more fuel, nearly doubling the weight of the vehicle and making it difficult to reach space. For this reason, it was important to develop the WK to take SS1 up to about 47,000 feet (14,000 metres) and drop it from underneath. The SS1 pilot would then light the hybrid rocket, which would send SS1 into a near-vertical trajectory.

A unique feature of SS1 that made the flights possible was its "feather" system. After the rocket finished its burn and before SS1 reached its highest point, the pilot would extend the feather; that is, the rear half of the wings of SS1 would fold vertically to a "shuttlecock" position, increasing drag to reduce speed and thermal load for reentry. After reentry, the pilot would retract the feather and bring the craft into a glider formation, landing smoothly at low speed.

A series of test flights took place to verify the systems of the WK and SS1. The cabin layout for WK was identical to that of SS1, allowing it to serve as a training platform for the space vehicle. Flight testing of the WK began on Aug. 1, 2002. After 23 flights, the WK took SS1 to an altitude of 48,000 feet (15,000 metres) for its first captive-carry flight. SS1 completed three captive carries, nine glides, and three rocket-powered flights before attaining space.

SpaceShipOne's first rocket-powered flight was on Dec. 17, 2003—a date chosen by Scaled Composites management in tribute to the 100th anniversary of the Wright Brothers' first flight at Kitty Hawk. American test pilot Brian Binnie was at the controls as the SS1-mounted rocket was first ignited for a burn lasting 15 seconds. Reaching an altitude of 67,800 feet (20,700 metres) and supersonic speeds, SS1 had a fairly smooth trip until landing. Upon touchdown the left landing gear collapsed, sending SS1 into the dirt. There was little damage to the vehicle, however,

and, due to the ease of repairing composite structures, SS1 was able to execute a glide flight less than three months later.

With each successive flight, systems were tested and improved, gradually expanding the capabilities of the craft. Since SS1 was the first private space vehicle, there was a delay between the first and second rocket-powered flights, as it was necessary for Scaled Composites to be licensed by the Federal Aviation Administration's Office of Commercial Space Transportation (FAA AST) to extend the rocket burn beyond 15 seconds.

On April 8, 2004, American test pilot Pete Siebold took SS1 over 115,000 feet (35,000 metres) with a 40-second burn. One month later South African-born American test pilot Mike Melvill took the craft to 211,400 feet (64,400 metres) and Mach 2.5 (2.5 times the speed of sound) with a 55-second rocket burn.

SS1 rocketed into the record books on June 21, 2004. With Melvill at the controls, SS1 was able to squeeze past the edge of space with only 491 feet (150 metres) to spare, thus becoming the first private manned space vehicle and making its pilot the first commercial astronaut-pilot. (The FAA AST created special wings to commemorate these pioneers.) Melvill celebrated the event by releasing chocolate candy in the cabin during his 3.5 minutes of weightlessness.

Having proved that the vehicle could accomplish the goals as set forth for the Ansari X Prize, dates were scheduled for the first flight of the competition. On Sept. 29, 2004, with Melvill again piloting the craft, SS1 attained 337,700 feet (102,900 metres). Thousands were watching as the craft experienced a series of vertical rolls during the rocket boost that were corrected by the pilot. Indeed, all three of Melvill's flights experienced anomalies that he was able to correct with his fly-by-wire skills and assistance from the ground crew.

The second Ansari X Prize flight was flown on Oct. 4, 2004. Pilot Brian Binnie achieved a new apogee milestone of 367,500 feet (112,000 metres), surpassing the X-15 rocket plane's altitude record by 13,000 feet (4,000 metres). Like Melvill, Binnie took advantage of the weightlessness to fly a paper SS1 around the cockpit. Both pilots experienced high gravity forces (*g*-forces) on the return, up to 5.4 *g*, and were able to bring the craft back into glider formation for a smooth landing.

SS1 now hangs in the Smithsonian Institution's National Air and Space Museum in Washington, D.C., a monument to the future of space tourism. In winning the Ansari X Prize, SpaceShipOne ushered in a new era of commercial manned spaceflight and space tourism.

Regulating Space Tourism

In 2004 the U.S. Commercial Space Launch Amendments Act (CSLAA) provided guidelines for regulating the safety of commercial human spaceflight in the United States under the auspices of the Federal Aviation Administration (FAA). Under the CSLAA, FAA representatives will attend every launch, evaluate every landing, and work alongside the space tourism operators; however, the FAA will not be permitted to impose any safety regulations until 2012 unless there is a serious incident.

The guidelines also require space tourism operators to inform spaceflight participants in writing about the risks of launch and reentry and about the safety record of the launch vehicle. The CSLAA guidelines also require spaceflight participants to provide informed consent to participate in launch and reentry.

At this early stage in the development of the suborbital space tourism industry, it is difficult for the FAA to control how companies design their vehicles or to assess the safety of launching spaceflight participants into space. Despite safety concerns, Virgin Galactic has sold more than 200 seats at $200,000 each for its suborbital space tourism flights, which are scheduled to commence in early 2010. Carrying Virgin Galactic's spaceflight participants into space will be SpaceShipTwo, which will be launched from a permanent spaceport near Upham, N.M.

Virgin Galactic is not alone in its interest in space tourism, an industry that may prove to be especially lucrative in the 21st century. For example, Astrium, a subsidiary of European aerospace giant European Aeronautic Defence and Space Company, announced its own space tourism project in June 2007. The Astrium project is the first entry into space tourism by a major aerospace contractor and features a rocket plane with a large wingspan and a pair of canards. Development of the rocket plane commenced in 2008, with the objective of the first suborbital flight in 2011. The ticket price of $250,000 will include a round-trip to the spaceport (located in Tunisia), spaceflight participant training, luxury resort accommodation, and a thrilling Mach 3 ride into space.

Competing with Virgin Galactic and Astrium is XCOR Aerospace, a California company that in 2008 unveiled the Lynx, a suborbital spaceship that will provide front-seat rides into space by 2010. In Texas, Blue Origin, a privately funded aerospace company set up by Amazon.com founder Jeff Bezos, has developed its New Shepard spacecraft (named for American astronaut Alan Shepard), scheduled to commence a weekly suborbital tourist service to space in 2010. With its bullet-shaped fuselage, New Shepard is designed to take off and land vertically, in contrast to the conventional runway take-off and landing of the Astrium and XCOR rocket planes and the mother-ship deployment of SpaceShipTwo.

The efforts of Virgin Galactic, Astrium, XCOR, and Blue Origin represent just some of the developing space fleets projected to ferry tourists to and from space. Having overcome daunting technical challenges and significant financial constraints, these companies are on the threshold of opening the frontier of space to a much greater section of the population. As the space tourism industry evolves, the ranks of spaceflight participants will grow, and suborbital and orbital flights will inevitably give way to lunar excursions and trips to Mars and beyond, by which time space tourism will be operating as a full-fledged industry capable of truly opening the frontier of space.

CHAPTER 7

HUMANS IN SPACE

By 2009 more than 485 individuals, including 50 women, from nearly 40 different countries had been launched into orbit. Some individuals have made several separate flights. Those are particularly impressive numbers since, as of that same time, only the United States, Russia, and China had the capability of carrying out human spaceflights.

A more sobering number involves the men and women who have been lost while traveling through space. From the crash landing of the first manned Soyuz spacecraft in 1967 to the explosion of the shuttle orbiter *Columbia* in 2003, 18 people have died during spaceflights.

Human spaceflight is both risky and expensive. One feeds off the other. Providing the systems to support people while in orbit adds significant additional costs to a space mission, and ensuring that the launch, flight, and reentry are carried out as safely as possible also requires highly reliable and thus costly equipment, including both spacecraft and launchers.

From the start of human spaceflight efforts, people have weighed the inherent risks and benefits. Some have argued that the benefits of sending humans into space do not justify either the risks or the costs. They contend that robotic missions can produce equal or even greater scientific results with lower expenditures and that human presence in space has no other valid justification.

Those who support human spaceflight cite the still unmatched ability of human intelligence, flexibility, and reliability in carrying out certain experiments in orbit, in repairing and maintaining robotic spacecraft and automated instruments in space, and in acting as explorers in initial journeys to other places in the solar system. They also argue that astronauts serve as excellent role models for younger people and act as vicarious representatives of the many who would like to fly in space themselves. In addition is the long-held view that eventually some humans will leave Earth to establish permanent outposts and larger settlements on the Moon, Mars, or other locations.

The U.S. robotic rover Opportunity *traversing the Martian surface, as depicted in an artist's conception.* NASA/Goddard Space Flight Center

BIOMEDICAL, PSYCHOLOGICAL, AND SOCIOLOGICAL ASPECTS

Human beings have evolved to live in the environment of Earth's surface. The space environment—with its very low level of gravity, lack of atmosphere, wide temperature variations, and often high levels of ionizing radiation from the Sun, from particles trapped in the Van Allen radiation belts, and from cosmic rays—is an unnatural place for humans. An understanding of the effects on the human body of spaceflight, particularly long-duration flights away from Earth to destinations such as Mars, is incomplete.

A majority of those going into space experience space sickness, which may cause vomiting, nausea, and stomach discomfort, among other symptoms. The condition is thought to arise from a contradiction experienced in the brain between external information coming from the eyes and internal information coming from the balance organs in the inner ear, which are normally stimulated continually by gravity. Space sickness usually disappears within two or three days as the brain adapts to the space environment, although symptoms may reappear temporarily when the space traveler returns to Earth's gravity.

The virtual absence of gravity causes loss of tissue mass in the calf and thigh muscles, which are used on Earth's surface to counter the effect of gravity. Muscles that are less involved with gravity, such as those used to bend the legs or arms, are less affected. Some loss of muscle mass in the heart has been observed in astronauts on long-duration missions. In the absence of gravity, blood that normally pools in the body's lower extremities initially shifts to the upper regions. As a result, the face appears puffy, the person experiences sinus congestion and headaches, and blood production decreases as the body attempts to compensate. In addition, in the space environment, some weight-bearing bones in the body atrophy.

Although the changes in muscle, bone, and blood production do not pose problems for astronauts in space, they do so on their return to Earth. For example, in normal gravity, a person with decreased bone mass runs a greater risk of breaking a bone during normal strenuous activity. Countermeasures, particularly various forms of exercise while in space, have been developed to prevent these effects from causing health problems later on Earth. Even so, people recovering from long-duration flights require varying amounts of time to readjust to Earth conditions. Light-headedness usually disappears within one or two days; lack of balance and symptoms of motion sickness, in three to five days; anemia, in one to two weeks; muscle atrophy, in three to five weeks; and bone atrophy, in one to three years or more.

Except for the Apollo trips to the Moon, all human spaceflights have taken place in near-Earth orbit. In this location, Earth's magnetic field shields humans from potentially dangerous exposure to ionizing radiation from recurrent major disturbances on the Sun and interplanetary cosmic rays. The Apollo missions, which were all less than two weeks long, were timed to avoid exposure to anticipated high levels of solar radiation. If, however, humans were sent on journeys to Mars or other destinations that would take months or even years, such measures would be inadequate. Exposure to high levels of solar radiation or cosmic rays could cause potentially fatal tumours and other health problems.

Space engineers will need to devise adequate radiation shielding for interplanetary manned spacecraft and will require accurate predictions of radiation damage to the body to ensure that risks remain within acceptable limits. Biomedical advances are also necessary to develop methods for the early detection and mitigation of radiation damage. Nevertheless, the effects of radiation may remain a major obstacle to long human voyages in space.

In addition to the biomedical issues associated with human spaceflight are a number of psychological and sociological issues, particularly for long-duration missions aboard a space station or to distant destinations. To be in space is to be in an extreme and isolated environment. Mission planners will have to consider issues relating to crew size and composition—particularly if the crews are mixtures of men and women and come from several nations with different cultures—if interpersonal conflicts are to be avoided and effective teamwork achieved.

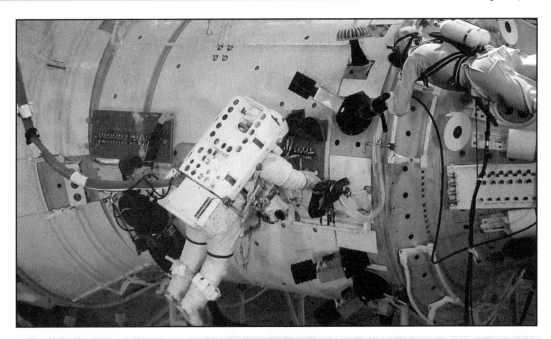

Spacesuited U.S. astronaut (centre), assisted by a scuba diver, practicing in-space assembly routines in a water-filled microgravity simulation tank at the Yury Gagarin Cosmonaut Training Centre (Star City) near Moscow. The rehearsal was part of preparations for a space shuttle mission to the International Space Station in September 2000. NASA

SELECTING PEOPLE FOR SPACEFLIGHT

Most of the individuals who have gone into space are highly trained astronauts and cosmonauts, the two designations having originated in the United States and the Soviet Union, respectively. (Both *taikonaut* and *yuhangyuan* have sometimes been used to describe the astronauts in China's manned space program.) Those governments interested in sending some of their citizens into space select candidates from many applicants, on the basis of their backgrounds and physical and psychological characteristics.

Candidates undergo rigorous training before being chosen for an initial spaceflight and then prepare in detail for each mission assigned. Training centres with specialized facilities exist in the United States, at NASA's Johnson Space Center, Houston, Texas; in Russia, at the Yury Gagarin Cosmonaut Training Centre (commonly called Star City), outside Moscow; in Germany, at ESA's European Astronaut Centre, Cologne; in Japan, at NASDA's Tsukuba Space Centre, near Tokyo; and in China, at Space City, near Beijing.

In both the United States and the Soviet Union, no women were initially selected

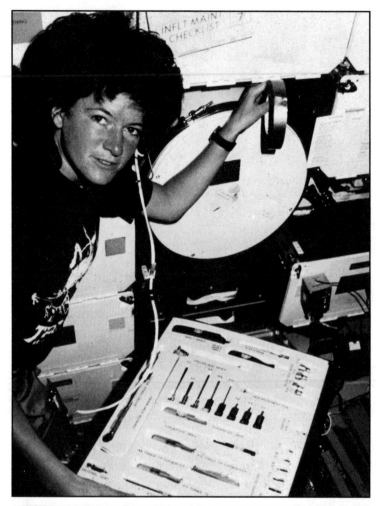

Sally Ride, the first U.S. female astronaut to fly into space, aboard the space shuttle Challenger *during her second flight in June 1983.* MPI/Hulton Archive/Getty Images

U.S. astronaut, Sally Ride, was launched aboard the space shuttle *Challenger* in June 1983.

The United States selected only pilots as astronauts until 1965, when six scientists with technical or medical degrees were chosen for astronaut training. One of them, geologist Harrison ("Jack") Schmitt, became a crew member of Apollo 17, the final Apollo mission to the Moon, in December 1972.

U.S. ASTRONAUT TRAINING

Even though initially most U.S. astronauts were test pilots, this requirement had more to do with their ability to perform effectively in high-stress situations than with their piloting skills, since the spacecraft used in the Mercury, Gemini, and Apollo programs had limited maneuvering capability in orbit and came back to Earth using parachutes for reentry. Since 1978, with the advent of the space shuttle, which functions as a laboratory and operations centre when in orbit and then as a high-speed, difficult-to-control glider as it reenters the atmosphere and flies to a

for spaceflight training. In 1962 the Soviet Union chose five women as cosmonaut trainees; one of them, Valentina Tereshkova, went into orbit in June 1963, becoming the first woman in space. The United States did not select women for astronaut training until 1978, and the first female

Robert L. Satcher, Jr., mission specialist astronaut candidate, floating freely aboard a KC-135 aircraft as part of his early training on Oct. 13, 2004. NASA

runway landing, NASA has selected two different types of individuals as astronaut candidates. One group is required to have extensive flying experience in jet aircraft. These astronaut candidates are trained to serve as shuttle pilots and eventually shuttle mission commanders. The second group is chosen to become mission specialist astronauts. These candidates are not required to be pilots (though some are); rather, they are individuals with advanced scientific, medical, or engineering training or experience. Since 1992, in anticipation of participating in missions to the International Space Station (ISS), a number of individuals from various countries have become international mission specialist astronaut candidates.

Mission specialists are trained to have primary responsibility during a mission for operating shuttle or space station systems and carrying out payload and experimental activities. Mission specialists also perform extravehicular activities (space walks). Another mission specialist category (added in 2002) is the educator mission specialist. These individuals are trained to go into space in support of educational activities on Earth.

Astronaut candidates can come from either civilian or military life. All (except the education mission specialist candidates) are required to have a college degree in engineering, life science or physical science, or mathematics. Both men and women are eligible to apply as either a pilot or a mission specialist candidate. A person wishing to become an astronaut must file a formal application with NASA and undergo a rigorous screening process consisting of personal interviews, medical evaluations, and orientation to the space program.

According to NASA, those selected are expected to be team players and highly skilled generalists with a certain degree of individuality and self-reliance. The average age of an individual selected as a NASA astronaut candidate has been

Richard R. Arnold II, educator mission specialist, simulating a parachute water landing in inclement weather during water survival training, June 21–25, 2004, at Pensacola Naval Air Station. NASA

in the mid-30s. The maximum height for an astronaut candidate is now 6 feet 4 inches (193 cm); the minimum height is 4 feet 10.5 inches (149 cm), though pilots must be at least 5 feet 4 inches (163 cm).

Astronaut candidates participate in an intense one-to-two-year training program. They learn shuttle and space station systems, guidance and navigation, orbital dynamics, and materials processing as well as mathematics, geology, meteorology, oceanography, astronomy, and physics. They are also trained in land and sea survival, scuba diving, space suits, and weightlessness. After successfully completing their training, candidates are designated NASA career astronauts.

In addition to pilots and mission specialist astronauts, who expect to fly on several space missions during their time at NASA, there is a third category of individuals who have gone into space on the shuttle. These individuals are designated payload specialists. The specialists are required to carry out experiments or payload activities with which they are particularly familiar. However, sometimes payload specialists have been individuals selected to go into space for political reasons, such as members of the U.S. Congress—during the 1980s two members of Congress, Sen. Jake Garn of Utah and Rep. Bill Nelson of Florida, flew aboard the space shuttle as payload specialists—or persons from countries allied with the United States.

Although they are known to the general public as astronauts, payload

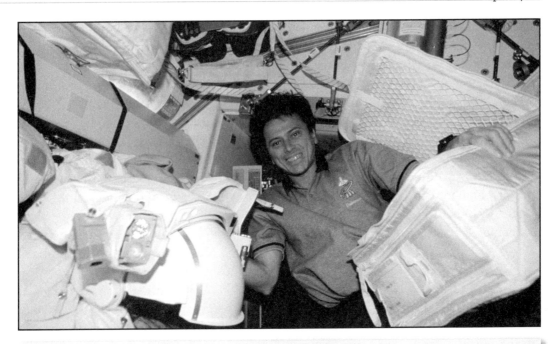

Astronaut Franklin R. Chang-Díaz in the International Space Station during transfer of supplies and equipment, June 2002. NASA

specialists do not undergo formal astronaut selection or training and are not designated NASA career astronauts. They must, however, have education and training appropriate to their mission responsibilities and must pass a physical examination. A payload specialist for a specific spaceflight is nominated by NASA, a non-U.S. space agency, or a payload sponsor. Teacher Christa McAuliffe was a "teacher in space" payload specialist on the doomed *Challenger* mission. The first U.S. astronaut to orbit Earth, John Glenn, returned to space as a shuttle payload specialist (and as the oldest person to make a spaceflight) in October 1998. The usual expectation is that a payload specialist will make only one spaceflight.

Once an astronaut is assigned to a particular mission, he or she and other members of the crew train together for a number of months to prepare themselves for the specific activities of their spaceflight. This can include Russian classes if they are to be part of a long-duration crew on the ISS. They use a variety of simulators and other equipment during their training to familiarize themselves with the planned mission activities and to react to simulated emergencies and other deviations from normal operations.

With the advent of long-duration missions on the ISS, the distinction between pilot astronauts and mission specialists has become less rigid; an astronaut from either group can be a candidate for assignment to a station mission. Currently, payload specialists are not eligible for long-duration flights. Between their spaceflight assignments, astronauts take on a variety of tasks within NASA, ranging from mission control communicators (maintaining contact with their colleagues in space) to senior managers.

COSMONAUT AND INTERNATIONAL ASTRONAUT TRAINING

In the Russian space program there have traditionally been two categories of cosmonauts—mission commanders (who are usually pilots) and flight engineers. As in the United States, cosmonaut candidates must undergo a rigorous physical examination, sometimes extending over several months, to assess their capability for long-duration flights. Training for cosmonaut candidates includes two years of general topics related to spaceflight, after which they are designated cosmonauts, and then up to two years of training on spaceflight hardware. Only then may an individual

be assigned to a specific mission, with one or more additional years of training required before launch.

In contrast to U.S. astronaut mission training, which until the late 1990s emphasized the specific tasks to be accomplished on a short space shuttle mission, formerly Soviet and now Russian training has emphasized the general spaceflight and problem-solving skills associated with longer stays in space. Since the late 1990s, U.S. astronaut training has moved toward a similar approach for those astronauts preparing to stay on the ISS in which the distinction between pilot and nonpilot astronauts and cosmonauts has become less clear because all members of a space station crew carry out station operations and experiments.

The 15-country European Space Agency, Japan, and Canada have programs for the selection and training of government-sponsored astronauts that are similar to those of NASA. Individuals selected by other countries to go into space participate in either the U.S. astronaut or Russian cosmonaut training program, or both. Those training for missions on the ISS may also visit locations in Europe, Japan, and Canada for specialized training related to space station hardware.

CHAPTER 8

AMERICAN ASTRONAUTS

They are pioneers of a new frontier. Even before they were launched into space, many of the early United States astronauts were already considered heroes for their service as military fighter and test pilots. The tradition of recruiting elite pilots and promising Air Force and Naval Academy graduates to the space program has continued into the present day. Joining them are aerospace engineers, electronics specialists, astrophysicists—even a teacher or two.

The background, accomplishments, and life after space of these brave men and women provide key insights into what it takes to be a space explorer.

Astronaut Edwin ("Buzz") Aldrin, Jr., pilot of the Gemini 12 spacecraft, practicing extravehicular work during underwater zero-gravity training. NASA/Johnson Space Center Collection

EDWIN "BUZZ" ALDRIN

(b. Jan. 20, 1930, Montclair, N.J., U.S.)

Astronaut Edwin ("Buzz") Aldrin, Jr., pilot of the Gemini 12 spacecraft, performing an extra-vehicular activity (EVA) on Nov. 12, 1966, the second day of the four-day mission in space. Aldrin is positioned next to the Agena workstation. **NASA** Great Images in Nasa Collection

Edwin Eugene "Buzz" Aldrin, Jr., set a record for extravehicular activity and was the second man to set foot on the Moon. A graduate of the U.S. Military Academy, West Point, N.Y. (1951), Aldrin became an air force pilot. He flew 66 combat missions in Korea and later served in West Germany.

In 1963 he wrote a dissertation on orbital mechanics to earn his Ph.D. from the Massachusetts Institute of Technology, Cambridge. Later that year he was chosen as an astronaut. On Nov. 11, 1966, he joined James A. Lovell, Jr., on the four-day Gemini 12 flight. Aldrin's 5 ½-hour walk in space proved that man can function effectively in the vacuum of space.

Apollo 11, manned by Aldrin, Neil A. Armstrong, and Michael Collins, was launched to the Moon on July 16, 1969. Four days later, Armstrong and Aldrin landed near the edge of Mare Tranquillitatis (Sea of Tranquillity). After

Apollo 11 astronaut Edwin Aldrin with the Lunar Module in the background, photograph by Neil Armstrong. NASA

spending about two hours gathering rock samples, taking photographs, and setting up scientific equipment for tests, the astronauts concluded their excursion on the surface. Armstrong and Aldrin later piloted the Lunar Module to a successful rendezvous with Collins and the Command Module in lunar orbit. The mission ended on July 24, with splashdown in the Pacific Ocean.

Aldrin retired from NASA in 1971 to become commandant of the Aerospace Research Pilots' School at Edwards Air Force Base, Calif. In March 1972 he retired from the air force to enter private business. He wrote an autobiographical book, *Return to Earth* (1973).

WILLIAM ANDERS
(b. Oct. 17, 1933, Hong Kong)

William Alison Anders participated in the Apollo 8 flight (Dec. 21–27, 1968), in which the first manned voyage around the Moon was made. The astronauts, including Anders, Frank Borman, and James Lovell, remained in an orbit about 70 miles (112 km) above the surface of the Moon for about 20 hours, transmitting television pictures back to Earth and verifying that lunar landmarks could be used for navigation to lunar landing sites.

Anders resigned from NASA and the air force in 1969 to become executive secretary of the National Aeronautics and Space Council. He served as a member of the Atomic Energy Commission (1973–74) and of the Nuclear Regulatory Commission (1974–76); as U.S. ambassador to Norway (1976–77); and as general manager of the Nuclear Products Division of General Electric Company (from 1977).

MICHAEL ANDERSON
(b. Dec. 25, 1959, Plattsburgh, N.Y., U.S.—d. Feb. 1, 2003, over Texas)

Michael Philip Anderson was the payload commander and a mission specialist on the space shuttle *Columbia*, when it broke up in the atmosphere over Texas. Anderson was educated at the University of Washington and at Creighton University, Omaha, Neb., where he earned a master's degree in physics. In 1991–95 he served in the U.S. Air Force as an instructor pilot and tactical officer, and in 1998 he flew in the space shuttle *Endeavour* on a mission to the Russian space station Mir.

NEIL ARMSTRONG
(b. Aug. 5, 1930, Wapakoneta, Ohio, U.S.)

Neil Alden Armstrong was the first person to set foot on the Moon. Armstrong became a licensed pilot on his 16th birthday and a naval air cadet in 1947. His studies in aeronautical engineering at Purdue University in West Lafayette, Ind., were interrupted in 1950 by the Korean War, in which he was shot down once and was awarded three Air Medals. In 1955 he became a civilian research pilot for the National Advisory Committee for Aeronautics (NACA), later NASA. He flew more than 1,100 hours, testing various supersonic fighters as well as the X-15 rocket plane.

In 1962 he joined the space program with the second group of astronauts. On March 16, 1966, Armstrong, as command pilot of Gemini 8, and David R. Scott rendezvoused with an unmanned Agena rocket and completed the first manual space-docking maneuver. After the docking, a rocket-thruster malfunction forced them to separate from the Agena. Armstrong then regained control of the Gemini craft and made an emergency splashdown in the Pacific Ocean.

On July 16, 1969, Armstrong, along with Edwin E. Aldrin, Jr., and Michael Collins, blasted off in the Apollo 11 vehicle toward the Moon. Four days later, at 4:18 PM U.S. Eastern Daylight Time (EDT), the Eagle lunar landing module, guided manually by Armstrong, touched down on a plain near the southwestern edge of the Sea of Tranquillity (Mare Tranquillitatis). At 10:56 PM EDT on July 20, 1969, Armstrong stepped from the Eagle onto the Moon's dusty surface with the words, "That's one small step for [a] man, one giant leap for mankind." (In the excitement of the moment, Armstrong skipped the "a" in the statement that he had prepared.) Armstrong and Aldrin left the module for more than two hours and deployed scientific instruments, collected surface samples, and took numerous photographs.

On July 21, after 21 hours and 36 minutes on the Moon, they lifted off to rendezvous with Collins and begin the voyage back to Earth. After splashdown in the Pacific at 12:51 PM EDT on July 24, the three astronauts spent 18 days in quarantine to guard against possible contamination by lunar microbes. During the days that followed and during a tour of 21 nations, they were hailed for their part in the opening of a new era in mankind's exploration of the universe.

Neil Armstrong poses prior to making history as the first man to set foot on the Moon. The 1969 Apollo 11 mission began a new era in space exploration. NASA/Getty Images

Armstrong resigned from NASA in 1971. From 1971 to 1979 he was professor of aerospace engineering at the University of Cincinnati (Ohio). After 1979 Armstrong served as chairman or director for a number of companies. He also sat on the National Commission on Space (NCOS), a panel charged with setting goals for the space program, and on the Presidential Commission on the Space Shuttle Challenger Accident, the group appointed in 1986 to analyze the safety failures in the *Challenger* disaster.

ALAN BEAN

(b. March 15, 1932, Wheeler, Texas, U.S.)

Alan LaVern Bean participated in the Apollo 12 mission (Nov. 14–22, 1969), during which two long walks totaling nearly eight hours were made on the Moon's surface. Bean and Comdr. Charles Conrad, Jr., piloted the Lunar Module to a pinpoint landing on the Moon while astronaut Richard F. Gordon, Jr., orbited overhead in the Command Module.

Bean entered the U.S. Navy upon graduation (1955) from the University of Texas, Austin, and served as a test pilot before entering the manned spaceflight program in 1963. In addition to the Apollo 12 mission, Bean was

Alan Bean, 1969. Courtesy of the National Aeronautics and Space Administration

commander of the Skylab 3 mission (July 28–Sept. 25, 1973), during which he, Owen K. Garriott, and Jack R. Lousma formed the second crew to occupy the orbiting laboratory.

Bean retired from the navy in 1975 but remained with NASA as chief of the astronaut candidate operations and training group.

The crew of the Apollo 12 lunar landing mission: (left to right) *Charles ("Pete") Conrad, Jr.; Richard F. Gordon, Jr.; and Alan L. Bean.* NASA Great Images in Nasa Collection

GUION BLUFORD

(b. Nov. 22, 1942, Philadelphia, Pa., U.S.)

Guion Stewart Bluford, Jr., was the first African American launched into space. Bluford received an undergraduate degree in aerospace engineering from Pennsylvania State University in 1964 and was commissioned as an officer in the U.S. Air Force, where he trained as a fighter pilot. He flew 144 combat missions during the Vietnam War. In 1978 he earned a doctorate in aerospace engineering from the Air Force Institute of Technology.

Bluford was one of 35 individuals selected in 1978 from 10,000 applicants in NASA's first competition to become space shuttle astronauts. On Aug. 30, 1983, he rode into Earth orbit on the shuttle orbiter *Challenger*; he subsequently flew on three additional shuttle missions between 1985 and 1992. Bluford served as a mission specialist on all four flights, with responsibility for a variety of in-orbit tasks, including the deployment of an Indian communications satellite as well as the operation and deployment of scientific and classified military experiments and payloads.

Guion S. Bluford, Jr., exercising on a treadmill aboard the U.S. space shuttle Challenger *in Earth orbit, 1983.* NASA

In 1987 Bluford received a graduate degree in business administration from the University of Houston, Clear Lake. He left NASA in July 1993 for a private-sector career in the information technology and engineering services field.

FRANK BORMAN
(b. March 14, 1928, Gary, Ind., U.S.)

Frank Borman, with James A. Lovell and William A. Anders, made the first manned flight around the Moon in Apollo 8 in December 1968. Three years earlier Borman and Lovell had made the Gemini 7

Frank Borman, 1964. NASA/Johnson Space Center

endurance flight in which they remained in space for 330 hours 35 minutes.

Borman graduated from the U.S. Military Academy, West Point, N.Y., in 1950, was commissioned in the air force, and served with the 44th Fighter Bomber Squadron in the Philippines between 1951 and 1956. He subsequently taught at the Air Force Fighter Weapons School. After taking his master's degree in aeronautical engineering (1957) at California Institute of Technology, Pasadena, Borman taught at West Point and at the Air Force Aerospace Research Pilots School. In 1962 he was chosen by NASA to be a member of the second group of astronauts. After the Apollo 8 flight he became deputy director of flight-crew operations for NASA.

In July 1970 Borman resigned from NASA and became a company executive of Eastern Air Lines (1970–86).

VANCE BRAND
(b. May 9, 1931, Longmont, Colo., U.S.)

Vance DeVoe Brand was command pilot for several historic space ventures, including the first joint U.S.-Soviet manned space mission and the first fully operational space shuttle mission.

Brand gained flight experience as an aviator with the U.S. Marine Corps Reserve from 1953 to 1957 and graduated from the U.S. Naval Test Pilot School, Patuxent, Md., in 1963. He subsequently worked as an engineering test pilot for the Lockheed Company until 1966, when NASA chose him to be an astronaut.

Brand was backup command module pilot for Apollo 15 and backup commander for the Skylab 3 and 4 missions prior to being named command pilot for the Apollo-Soyuz Test Project (ASTP).

The ASTP involved the rendezvous (July 15–24, 1975) in Earth orbit of an Apollo craft with a Soyuz space capsule. After docking together, the combined crews conducted scientific experiments. Brand was the commander on the fifth space shuttle flight (STS-5; Nov. 11–16, 1982), on which the shuttle *Columbia* first launched two satellites into orbit. On his third space mission, Brand was commander of the *Challenger* space shuttle (STS-41-B; Feb. 3–11, 1984). Although this trip was plagued by several malfunctions and two communications satellites were misdirected, Bruce McCandless's performance of the first space walk without a lifeline and the successful return of the shuttle to its home base were regarded as major accomplishments. Brand's fourth space mission (STS-35; Dec. 2–10, 1990) carried the ASTRO-1 observatory, which consisted of three ultraviolet telescopes and one X-ray telescope.

Brand left the astronaut corps in 1992, but he continued to work with NASA in a variety of positions, mainly at the Dryden Flight Research Center in Edwards, Calif., until his retirement in 2008.

DAVID BROWN

(b. April 16, 1956, Arlington, Va., U.S.—d. Feb. 1, 2003, over Texas)

David McDowell Brown was a mission specialist and flight surgeon on the space shuttle *Columbia*'s final flight. Brown was educated at the College of William and Mary, Williamsburg, Va., and at Eastern Virginia Medical School, where he earned a doctorate in medicine in 1982. He was director of medical services at the Navy Branch Hospital in Adak, Alaska, and served on an aircraft carrier before beginning pilot training in 1988; he was chosen for the astronaut program in 1996.

SCOTT CARPENTER

(b. May 1, 1925, Boulder, Colo., U.S.)

Malcolm Scott Carpenter was the second American astronaut to make an orbital

M. Scott Carpenter, 1964. Courtesy of the National Aeronautics and Space Administration

spaceflight. In *Aurora 7* he made the fourth Mercury flight, circling Earth three times on May 24, 1962. He directed part of the flight by manual control.

Carpenter entered the U.S. Navy in 1949 and served in the Korean War. He had been a navy test pilot and had attended the Naval Air Intelligence School in 1958. He was one of seven men selected in April 1959 for NASA's Project Mercury. In 1964 he broke his left arm in a motorcycle accident. The resultant inability to rotate his arm properly forced his removal from spaceflight status.

In 1965 Carpenter was detached from the space program to lead two teams in the Sealab II experiment, living and working 205 feet (62.5 metres) under the Pacific Ocean as part of the U.S. Navy's effort to find better rescue methods for submarines. In 1967 he helped set up Sealab III but retired from naval duty in 1969 to enter private oceanography and energy research.

GERALD CARR
(b. Aug. 22, 1932, Denver, Colo., U.S.)

Gerald Paul Carr commanded the Skylab 4 mission, which established a new manned spaceflight record of 84 days. Carr graduated from the University of Southern California, Los Angeles, in 1954 with a degree in mechanical engineering. Later that same year he joined the U.S. Marine Corps and advanced to the rank of colonel. He continued his education at the U.S. Naval Postgraduate School, where he received a second bachelor's degree in 1962, this time in aeronautical engineering. After pursuing advanced studies in the same field at Princeton University, he entered the astronaut program in 1966. He played a key role in the development of the lunar rover, a vehicle used on the Apollo 15, 16, and 17 missions to explore the Moon's surface.

Skylab 4, launched on Nov. 16, 1973, proved that humans could live and work in the weightless conditions of space for an extended period of time. The three-man crew comprised Carr, science pilot Edward Gibson, and command module pilot William Pogue. They made close-up observations of comet Kohoutek, the first above-atmosphere study of a comet ever conducted.

Carr retired from the Marine Corps in 1975 and resigned from the astronaut program two years later to enter private industry. In 1984 he founded Camus, a company that provided technical support in the design of the International Space Station. He retired from Camus in 1998.

EUGENE CERNAN
(b. March 14, 1934, Chicago, Ill., U.S.)

Eugene Andrew Cernan left his spacecraft for more than two hours of extravehicular activity during the Gemini 9 mission (1966) and was the last man on the Moon.

Cernan was commissioned in the U.S. Navy in 1956, became a test pilot, and earned his master's degree in aeronautical engineering at the U.S. Naval

Eugene Andrew Cernan, 1964. NASA

a complex series of orbital maneuvers before rejoining the Command Module. The mission performed every function necessary for a lunar landing but the landing itself and was the final test of Apollo systems.

Cernan commanded the Apollo 17 Moon flight (with Ronald Evans and Harrison Schmitt, Dec. 7–19, 1972). He and Schmitt, a geologist, explored the Taurus-Littrow region of the Moon's surface (December 11–14) and concluded the Apollo Moon program. After serving as deputy director of the Apollo-Soyuz Test Project (completed in July 1975), Cernan resigned from the navy and the space program in 1976 to enter private business.

Postgraduate School, Monterey, Calif. In 1963 he was named in the second group of astronauts.

Cernan and Thomas P. Stafford were launched into space on June 3, 1966, in Gemini 9. In addition to the activity outside the craft, they rendezvoused three times with a target vehicle during the three-day mission.

On May 18, 1969, Cernan, Stafford, and John W. Young began the eight-day mission of Apollo 10. As lunar module pilot, Cernan brought the landing craft into a close lunar orbit, approaching the surface to within 16 km (10 miles). Stafford and Cernan completed

ROGER CHAFFEE

(b. Feb. 15, 1935, Grand Rapids, Mich., U.S.—d. Jan. 27, 1967, Cape Kennedy, Fla.)

Roger Bruce Chaffee was a member of the three-man Apollo 1 crew killed when a flash fire swept their space capsule during a simulation of a launching scheduled for Feb. 21, 1967. Chaffee died along with the veteran space travelers Virgil I. Grissom and Edward H. White II. They were the first casualties of the U.S. space program.

After earning his B.S. in aeronautical engineering from Purdue University, West Lafayette, Ind., in 1957, Chaffee became a navy pilot. He was chosen as one of the third group of astronauts in 1963.

Chang-Díaz made seven spaceflights. His first mission was aboard the space shuttle *Columbia* in January 1986. Other shuttle flights included the *Atlantis* mission in October 1989, which deployed the *Galileo* spacecraft that explored Jupiter, and the June 2002 flight of *Endeavour*, during which he participated in three space walks to help repair the robotic arm of the International Space Station. Chang-Díaz was a visiting scientist (1983–93) at MIT, where he led a project that developed plasma propulsion for use in human flights to Mars. He served as director of NASA's Advanced Space Propulsion Laboratory at the Johnson Space Center in Houston from 1993 until 2005, when he retired from the agency.

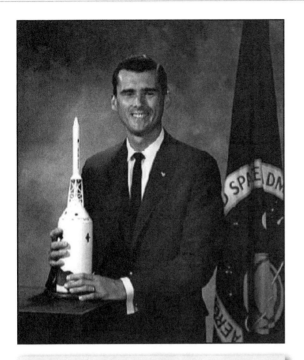

Roger B. Chaffee, 1964. NASA/Johnson Space Center

FRANKLIN CHANG-DÍAZ

(b. April 5, 1950, San José, Costa Rica)

Physicist Franklin Chang-Díaz was the first Hispanic American astronaut. Chang-Díaz aspired to be an astronaut as a young child. In 1967 his parents sent him from Costa Rica to live with relatives in Connecticut. He earned a bachelor's degree (1973) in mechanical engineering at the University of Connecticut and a doctorate (1977) in applied plasma physics from the Massachusetts Institute of Technology (MIT).

In 1980 he was selected to participate in NASA's astronaut program.

KALPANA CHAWLA

(b. July 1, 1961, Karnal, India—d. Feb. 1, 2003, over Texas, U.S.)

Indian-born American astronaut Kalpana Chawla was a mission specialist on the space shuttle *Columbia*'s final flight. Chawla was the first woman to study aeronautical engineering at Punjab Engineering College; she continued her education at the University of Texas at Arlington and the University of Colorado at Boulder, where she earned a doctorate in aeronautical engineering (1988). She first flew on the *Columbia* in 1997 as a mission specialist and primary robotic arm operator.

LAUREL CLARK

(b. March 10, 1961, Ames, Iowa, U.S.—d. Feb. 1, 2003, over Texas)

Laurel Blair Salton Clark was a mission specialist and flight surgeon on the final flight of the space shuttle *Columbia*, when it was destroyed during reentry. Clark was educated at the University of Wisconsin at Madison, where she earned a doctorate in medicine in 1987. In the U.S. Navy she served as a diving medical officer and headed a submarine squadron medical SEAL unit before becoming a flight surgeon; she was chosen for the astronaut program in 1996.

EILEEN COLLINS

(b. Nov. 19, 1956, Elmira, N.Y., U.S.)

Eileen Collins was the first woman to pilot and, later, to command a space shuttle. Collins's love of airplanes and flying began as a child. At age 19 she saved money earned from part-time jobs and began taking flying lessons.

Collins graduated with a bachelor's degree in mathematics and economics from Syracuse (New York) University in 1978. She then became one of four women admitted to Air Force Undergraduate Pilot Training at Vance Air Force Base in Oklahoma. The first women astronauts

Eileen Collins toys with a roll of paper scrap in microgravity while serving as pilot of the U.S. space shuttle orbiter Atlantis *in May 1997.* NASA

were doing their parachute training at the same base at that time, and Collins realized that the goal of becoming an astronaut was within reach. In 1979 she became the air force's first female flight instructor and for the next 11 years taught both flying and math.

As a C-141 Starlifter transport aircraft commander, Collins participated in the U.S.-led invasion of Grenada in 1983, delivering troops and evacuating medical students. She continued her training at the Air Force Institute of Technology and was one of the first women to attend Air Force Test Pilot School, from which she graduated in 1990. She eventually achieved the air force rank of colonel. She also earned an M.S. in operations research from Stanford University in 1986 and an M.A. in space systems management from Webster University, St. Louis, Mo., in 1989.

Selected as an astronaut in 1990, Collins became the first woman pilot of a U.S. space shuttle in February 1995, serving on the orbiter *Discovery* for a rendezvous and docking mission to the Russian space station Mir. She piloted a second shuttle flight in May 1997, successfully docking the *Atlantis* with Mir to transfer personnel, equipment, and supplies. With hundreds of hours in space to her credit, Collins became the first woman to command a shuttle mission in July 1999, taking *Columbia* into Earth orbit to deploy the Chandra X-ray Observatory.

After *Columbia* was destroyed on a subsequent flight in February 2003, the entire shuttle fleet was grounded until July 2005, when Collins commanded *Discovery* on a "return to flight" mission to test new safety modifications and to resupply the International Space Station (ISS). Prior to *Discovery*'s docking with the ISS, Collins guided the spacecraft through a full 360° pitch (nose-over-tail) maneuver—the first person to do so with an orbiter—which allowed ISS crew members to photograph the spacecraft's belly for possible damage.

MICHAEL COLLINS
(b. Oct. 31, 1930, Rome, Italy)

Michael Collins was copilot of the Gemini 10 flight and command module pilot of Apollo 11, the first manned lunar landing mission. A graduate of the U.S. Military Academy at West Point, N.Y., Collins transferred to the air force, becoming a test pilot at Edwards Air Force Base in California. He joined the space program in 1963.

Gemini 10, manned by Collins and John W. Young, was launched on July 18, 1966. After a rendezvous with an Agena target vehicle, the two men used the Agena's engines to propel them to a record altitude of 475 miles (764 km), where Collins left the spacecraft to remove equipment needed for a micrometeorite experiment from the aft end of the Gemini and attempted unsuccessfully to attach similar equipment to the Agena. He succeeded in retrieving an instrument from the Agena, but his activity was cut short because the Gemini

Michael Collins, 1969. NASA/Johnson Space Center

craft was low on fuel. Gemini 10 returned to Earth on July 21.

Collins participated in the Apollo 11 mission with Neil A. Armstrong and Edwin E. Aldrin, Jr. On July 20, 1969, Armstrong and Aldrin landed on the Moon. Collins remained in the Command Module, circling the Moon at an altitude of 60 to 75 miles (97 to 121 km). On July 21 Armstrong and Aldrin rejoined him, and the following day the astronauts left lunar orbit, landing in the Pacific Ocean on July 24. (His account of the landing,

Carrying the Fire, was published in 1974.) Apollo 11 was his last space mission; later in 1969 he was appointed assistant secretary of state for public affairs. In 1971 he joined the administrative staff of the Smithsonian Institution, Washington, D.C.

CHARLES CONRAD
(b. June 2, 1930, Philadelphia, Pa., U.S.—d. July 8, 1999, near Ojai, Calif.)

Charles P. "Pete" Conrad, Jr., was copilot on the Gemini 5 spaceflight (1965), command pilot of Gemini 11, spacecraft commander of the Apollo 12 flight to the Moon, and commander of the Skylab 2 mission.

Conrad enlisted in the U.S. Navy in 1953 and became a test pilot and flight instructor. In 1962 he was chosen as a member of the second group of astronauts. With command pilot L. Gordon Cooper, Jr., he took part in several new experiments during the Gemini 5 flight, which established a new manned-spaceflight record of 190 hours 56 minutes.

Manned by Conrad and Richard F. Gordon, Jr., Gemini 11 was launched on Sept. 12, 1966, and docked with an Agena target vehicle on the first orbit. The craft then attained a record manned orbit of 850 miles (1,370 km) altitude.

On Nov. 14, 1969, Conrad joined Gordon and Alan L. Bean on the Apollo 12 flight to the Moon. The success of the flight was characterized by the pinpoint landing (November 19) of the Lunar Module only 600 feet (183 m) from the unmanned Surveyor 3 craft, which had landed in April 1967. The total time spent on the lunar surface was 31 hours 31 minutes; Apollo 12 completed its return trip to Earth on November 24.

On the Skylab 2 mission (May 25–June 22, 1973) Conrad, Joseph P. Kerwin, and Paul J. Weitz docked their Apollo spacecraft with the orbiting Skylab, which had sustained damage during its launch on May 14. They made repairs to keep Skylab from overheating and to ensure a power supply sufficient to allow them to complete most of their assigned experimental work.

Conrad resigned from the navy and the space program in 1974, taking executive positions, first with the American Television and Communications Corporation of Denver, Colo., and in 1978 with the McDonnell-Douglas Corporation in Long Beach, Calif.

GORDON COOPER
(b. March 6, 1927, Shawnee, Okla., U.S.—d. Oct. 4, 2004, Ventura, Calif.)

Leroy Gordon Cooper, Jr., was one of the original team of seven American astronauts. On May 15–16, 1963, he circled Earth 22 times in the space capsule *Faith 7*, completing the sixth and last of the Mercury manned spaceflights. At the end of his 34-hour 20-minute flight, when the automatic control system had broken down, he piloted his craft back to Earth manually and landed just 4 miles (6 km) from the primary recovery ship. In August 1965 he served as command pilot of Gemini 5 on an eight-day endurance mission, becoming the first person to make two orbital flights.

After brief service with the Marine Corps, Cooper earned a commission with the U.S. Army at the University of Hawaii in Honolulu (1946–49) and transferred to the air force. He received a B.S. in aeronautics (1956) from the Air Force Institute of Technology, Wright-Patterson Air Force Base, Ohio, and served as a test pilot at Edwards Air Force Base, Calif., until 1959, when he was selected as a Mercury astronaut.

After serving as the backup pilot for *Sigma 7*'s 1962 mission, Cooper took his first spaceflight in May 1963. It was the longest of the Mercury flights, and with it Cooper became the last U.S. astronaut to fly alone. In 1965 Cooper flew with Charles Conrad, Jr., on Gemini 5. Although the mission was plagued by mechanical problems, they were able to set an endurance record of nearly 191 hours.

Cooper resigned from the air force and the space program in 1970 and entered private business. His autobiography, *Leap of Faith: An Astronaut's Journey into the Unknown*, was published in 2000.

ROBERT CRIPPEN
(b. Sept. 11, 1937, Beaumont, Texas, U.S.)

Robert Laurel Crippen served as pilot on the first U.S. space shuttle orbital flight.

Crippen graduated from the University of Texas, Austin, with a degree in

Robert Laurel Crippen, 1984. NASA/Johnson Space Center

aerospace engineering in 1960. He entered the U.S. Air Force Manned Orbiting Laboratory program in 1966 and transferred to the astronaut corps in 1969. He was named commander of the Skylab Medical Experiments Altitude Test several years later and was a member of the support crews for Skylab 2, 3, and 4 and the Apollo-Soyuz Test Project.

Manned by Crippen and John W. Young, the shuttle *Columbia*, the world's first reusable spacecraft, was launched on April 12, 1981. The two astronauts landed the airplane-like craft on April 14, after having orbited Earth 36 times. Crippen later commanded the second flight of the space shuttle *Challenger*. This flight (June 18–24, 1983) saw the first American woman in space, Sally Ride, and made Crippen the first to fly in two shuttle missions.

In 1984 he commanded two more shuttle flights. STS-41-C (*Challenger*, April 6–13, 1984) was the first mission in which a satellite, the malfunctioning Solar Maximum Mission, was repaired in Earth orbit. He then commanded STS-41-G (*Challenger*, Oct. 5–13, 1984), which was the first spaceflight with a seven-person crew and during which astronaut Kathryn Sullivan became the first American woman to walk in space.

From 1990 to 1992 he was director of the space shuttle program, and from 1992 to 1996 he was director of the Kennedy Space Center in Florida.

WALTER CUNNINGHAM
(b. March 16, 1932, Creston, Iowa, U.S.)

Ronnie Walter Cunningham was a civilian participant in the Apollo 7 mission (Oct. 11–22, 1968), in which the first manned flight of Apollo Command and Service modules was made.

Cunningham enlisted in the U.S. Navy in 1951 and transferred to the Marine Corps, where he served as a fighter pilot (1953–56). He majored in physics at the University of California, Los Angeles, receiving bachelor's (1960) and master's (1961) degrees but abandoning a doctoral program in favour of the manned space project in 1963. He left the space program in 1971 and became a corporation executive.

DONN EISELE
(b. June 23, 1930, Columbus, Ohio, U.S.—d. Dec. 2, 1987, Tokyo, Japan)

Donn Fulton Eisele served as command module pilot on the Apollo 7 mission (Oct. 11–22, 1968), the first manned flight of the Apollo program.

Eisele graduated from the U.S. Naval Academy, Annapolis, Md., in 1952 and transferred to the U.S. Air Force the next year. He received an M.S. in astronautics from the Air Force Institute of Technology at Wright-Patterson Air Force Base, Dayton, Ohio, in 1960, and he joined the space program in 1964. After completing the Apollo 7 mission, Eisele was named to the backup crew of Apollo 10. He left the astronaut corps in 1970 to take up an assignment at Langley Research Center in Hampton, Va.

Resigning from the air force and the space program in 1972, Eisele became director of the Peace Corps in Thailand and later accepted executive positions in private business enterprises.

OWEN GARRIOTT
(b. Nov. 22, 1930, Enid, Okla., U.S.)

Owen Kay Garriott was selected by NASA as one of the first scientist-astronauts. After completing a B.S. degree in electrical engineering from the University of Oklahoma in 1953, Garriott received an M.A. (1957) and a Ph.D. (1960), also in electrical engineering, from Stanford University. From 1953 to 1956 he served as an electronics officer in the U.S. Navy, and from 1961 to 1965 he taught in the department of electrical engineering at Stanford. In 1966 he qualified as a jet pilot.

After being accepted in NASA's scientist-astronaut program in 1965, Garriott went on two space missions. In 1973 he was the science pilot on Skylab 3, a 59-day mission to the Skylab space station that set a new record for the longest spaceflight. In 1983 he was a mission specialist on STS-9, a 10-day flight of the space shuttle *Columbia* that carried Spacelab, a science laboratory built by the European Space Agency. Between the two space missions, Garriott worked for the Lyndon B. Johnson Space Center in Houston, rising to the position of director of science and applications. From 1984 to 1986 he was project scientist in the Space Station Project Office.

Garriott later worked as a consultant for a variety of aerospace companies. From 1988 to 1993 he was vice president of space programs at Teledyne Brown Engineering. He received the NASA Distinguished Service Medal in 1973 and the NASA Space Flight Medal in 1983. His son, video-game developer Richard Garriott, became one of the first space tourists on a flight to the International Space Station in 2008 aboard Soyuz TMA-13.

EDWARD GIBSON
(b. Nov. 8, 1936, Buffalo, N.Y., U.S.)

Edward George Gibson was science pilot for the Skylab 4 mission, which established a new manned spaceflight record of 84 days.

Gibson received a doctorate in engineering from the California Institute of Technology (Caltech) in Pasadena in 1964. The next year he was selected to be an astronaut.

Skylab 4 was launched on Nov. 16, 1973, with a three-man crew: Gibson, commander Gerald Carr, and command module pilot William Pogue. Gibson used a set of special telescopes mounted on the orbiting space station to make detailed observations of the solar corona and chromosphere beyond the interference of Earth's atmosphere, producing much new data about the outer regions of the Sun and its activity cycle.

In 1974 he resigned from the astronaut program and became a senior staff scientist for the Aerospace Corporation, where he helped to analyze the solar data collected during the Skylab program. In 1977 Gibson rejoined the astronaut program and was assigned to the space shuttle project, but he resigned again in 1980 to enter private industry. He wrote a solar physics textbook, *The Quiet Sun* (1973), and two novels, *Reach* (1989) and *In the Wrong Hands* (1992).

JOHN GLENN
(b. July 18, 1921, Cambridge, Ohio, U.S.)

John Herschel Glenn, Jr., was the first American astronaut to orbit Earth,

Astronaut John H. Glenn, Jr., entering Friendship 7 *to begin the first American manned mission to orbit Earth, February 1962.* NASA

completing three orbits in 1962. (Soviet cosmonaut Yury Gagarin, the first person in space, made a single orbit of Earth in 1961).

Glenn joined the U.S. Marine Corps in 1943 and flew 59 missions during World War II and 90 missions during the Korean War. He was a test pilot from 1954 and was promoted to lieutenant colonel in 1959. Of the seven U.S. military pilots selected in that year for Project Mercury astronaut training, he was the oldest. Glenn served as a backup pilot for Alan B. Shepard, Jr., and Virgil I. Grissom, who made the first two U.S. suborbital flights into space. Glenn was selected for the first orbital flight, and on Feb. 20, 1962, his space capsule, *Friendship 7*, was

John H. Glenn, Jr. NASA

launched from Cape Canaveral, Fla. Its orbit ranged from approximately 99 to 162 miles (159 to 261 km) in altitude, and Glenn made three orbits, landing in the Atlantic Ocean near the Bahamas.

Glenn retired from the space program and the Marine Corps in 1964 to enter private business and to pursue his interest in politics. In 1970 he sought the Democratic nomination for a U.S. Senate seat in Ohio but lost narrowly in the primary. He was elected U.S. senator from that state in 1974 and was reelected three times thereafter. Glenn was unsuccessful, however, in his bid to become the 1984 Democratic presidential candidate.

On Oct. 29, 1998, Glenn returned to space as a payload specialist on a nine-day mission aboard the space shuttle *Discovery*. The oldest person ever to travel in space, Glenn at age 77 participated in experiments that studied similarities between the aging process and the body's response to weightlessness.

RICHARD GORDON
(b. Oct. 5, 1929, Seattle, Wash., U.S.)

Richard Francis Gordon, Jr., accompanied Charles Conrad on the September 1966 flight of Gemini 11. They docked with an Agena target on the first orbit and were propelled together to a record altitude of 850 miles (about 1,370 km). During a 45-minute space walk, Gordon joined the two crafts with a tether.

Gordon entered naval aviation training after he graduated from the University

Richard F. Gordon, Jr., 1964. NASA

of Washington, Seattle, in 1951. Six years later he became a test pilot, and in 1961 he won the Bendix Trophy Race, piloting an F4H Phantom jet from Los Angeles to New York City in the record time of 2 hours 47 minutes (an average speed of 879 miles [1,414 km] per hour).

In 1963 Gordon was chosen to be an astronaut. With Alan L. Bean and Charles Conrad, Gordon made the Apollo 12 flight, launched on Nov. 14, 1969. During this mission, the second manned landing on the Moon, Gordon was pilot of the Command Module and remained in lunar orbit during the lunar exploration. Gordon retired from the navy and the space program in 1972 and until 1977 served as executive vice president of

the New Orleans Saints, a professional gridiron-football team.

VIRGIL GRISSOM
(b. April 3, 1926, Mitchell, Ind., U.S.—d. Jan. 27, 1967, Cape Kennedy, Fla.)

Virgil Ivan "Gus" Grissom was the second American astronaut to travel in space and the command pilot of the ill-fated Apollo 1 crew. He and his fellow astronauts Edward H. White II and Roger B. Chaffee were killed, becoming the first casualties of the U.S. space program, when a flash fire swept their space capsule during a simulation of the scheduled Feb. 21, 1967, launching of Apollo 1.

Virgil I. Grissom, 1964. NASA

Commissioned in the U.S. Air Force in 1951, Grissom flew 100 missions in the Korean War, earning the Distinguished Flying Cross and the Air Medal with cluster. He was a test pilot and flying instructor until 1959, when he was selected as one of the original seven astronauts for Project Mercury. On July 21, 1961, Grissom became the third man to enter space, with a 15-minute suborbital journey aboard the space capsule *Liberty Bell 7*.

On March 23, 1965, Grissom became the first man to return to space, as he (as command pilot) and Lieutenant Commander John W. Young made three orbits in the first manned Gemini flight, Gemini 3. During that flight Grissom demonstrated that a space capsule could be maneuvered manually.

Astronauts John W. Young (left) and Virgil I. Grissom inside their Gemini 3 spacecraft awaiting blastoff from Cape Kennedy on March 23, 1965. They successfully orbited Earth three times in the first U.S. two-man spaceflight. NASA

FRED HAISE
(b. Nov. 14, 1933, Biloxi, Miss., U.S.)

Fred Wallace Haise, Jr., was a participant in the Apollo 13 mission (April 11–17, 1970), in which an intended Moon landing was canceled because of a rupture in a fuel-cell oxygen tank in the Service Module. The crew, consisting of Haise, John L. Swigert, Jr., and James A. Lovell, Jr., returned safely to Earth, however, making use of the life-support system in the Lunar Module.

Haise became a naval-aviation cadet in 1952 and served as a fighter pilot in the U.S. Marine Corps (1954–56). After obtaining a bachelor's degree (1959) from

Fred W. Haise, Jr., 1966. NASA

the University of Oklahoma, Norman, Haise joined NASA as a test pilot; he was selected for the manned space program in 1966.

After Project Apollo was closed in 1977, Haise was assigned to the space shuttle program for two years. He then accepted an executive position with the Grumman Aerospace Corporation, Bethpage, N.Y.

RICK HUSBAND
(b. July 12, 1957, Amarillo, Texas, U.S.—d. Feb. 1, 2003, over Texas)

Rick Douglas Husband was commander of the space shuttle *Columbia*'s final mission. Husband was educated at Texas Tech University and at California State University at Fresno, where he earned a master's degree in 1990. He joined the U.S. Air Force in 1980. In 1999 he flew on the *Discovery* on the first space shuttle mission to dock with the International Space Station.

JAMES IRWIN
(b. March 17, 1930, Pittsburgh, Pa., U.S.—d. Aug. 8, 1991, Glenwood Springs, Colo.)

James Benson Irwin was pilot of the Lunar Module on the Apollo 15 mission (July 26–Aug. 7, 1971), in which he and the mission commander, David R. Scott, spent almost three days on the Moon's surface investigating the Hadley-Apennine site, 462 miles (744 km) north of the lunar equator. The two spent 18 hours outside

James B. Irwin, 1966. NASA

the Lunar Module, traveled on the Moon's surface in a specially designed vehicle, and collected many rocks and core samples. Alfred M. Worden piloted the Command Module, orbiting the Moon while the others worked below.

Irwin graduated from the U.S. Naval Academy, Annapolis, Md., in 1951 and transferred to the air force. He earned a master's degree in aeronautical engineering at the University of Michigan, Ann Arbor, in 1957. At the time he was selected for the manned space program (1966), he was assigned to the Air Defense Command, Colorado Springs, Colo. The Apollo 15 flight was his only space mission.

Irwin resigned from the air force and the space program in 1972 to form and become president of High Flight Foundation, a Christian evangelical organization.

MAE JEMISON

(b. Oct. 17, 1956, Decatur, Ala., U.S.)

Physician Mae Carol Jemison was the first African American woman to become an astronaut. In 1992 she spent more than a week orbiting Earth in the space shuttle *Endeavour*.

Jemison moved with her family to Chicago at the age of three. There she was introduced to science by her uncle and developed interests throughout her childhood in anthropology, archaeology,

Mae Jemison aboard the space shuttle Endeavour. NASA/Marshall Space Flight Center

evolution, and astronomy. While still a high school student, she became interested in biomedical engineering, and after graduating in 1973, at the age of 16, she entered Stanford University. There she received degrees in chemical engineering and African American studies (1977).

In 1977 Jemison entered medical school at Cornell University in Ithaca, N.Y., where she pursued an interest in international medicine. After volunteering for a summer in a Cambodian refugee camp in Thailand, she studied in Kenya in 1979. She graduated from medical school in 1981, and, after a short time as a general practitioner with a Los Angeles medical group, she became a medical officer with the Peace Corps in West Africa. There she managed health care for Peace Corps and U.S. embassy personnel and worked in conjunction with the National Institutes of Health and the Centers for Disease Control on several research projects, including development of a hepatitis B vaccine.

After returning to the United States, Jemison applied to NASA to be an astronaut. In October 1986, she was 1 of 15 accepted out of 2,000 applicants. Jemison completed her training as a mission specialist with NASA in 1988. She became an astronaut office representative with the Kennedy Space Center at Cape Canaveral, Fla., working to process space shuttles for launching and to verify shuttle software. Next, she was assigned to support a cooperative mission between the United States and Japan designed to conduct experiments in materials processing and the life sciences. In September 1992, STS-47 Spacelab J became the first successful joint U.S.-Japan space mission.

Jemison's maiden space flight came with the week-long September 1992 mission of the shuttle *Endeavour*. At that time she was the only African American woman astronaut. After completing her NASA mission, she formed the Jemison Group, to develop and market advanced technologies.

JOSEPH KERWIN

(b. Feb. 19, 1932, Oak Park, Ill., U.S.)

Physician Joseph Peter Kerwin served as science pilot on Skylab 2, the first manned mission to the first U.S. space station.

Kerwin received his degree in medicine in 1957 from Northwestern University Medical School in Chicago, Ill., after which he joined the U.S. Navy Medical Corps. In 1965 NASA chose him to be an astronaut.

On May 14, 1973, the unmanned Skylab space station was launched but sustained serious damage in the process. One of Skylab's solar arrays was torn off; the other did not open. A sun shield designed to keep the station cool was also torn away, causing temperatures inside to reach 54 °C (129 °F). In an effort to save the space station, Kerwin, along with commander Charles Conrad, Jr., and command module pilot Paul Weitz, were launched on May 25, 1973, from Cape Kennedy to rendezvous with Skylab.

Kerwin helped repair the damaged space station and, as the first physician to participate in a U.S. spaceflight, monitored the physical effects (particularly of prolonged weightlessness) of the space environment on the crew. The astronauts successfully completed their mission and returned to Earth on June 22.

Kerwin subsequently worked at the astronaut office at the Johnson Space Center (JSC) in Houston, Texas. From 1982 to 1983 he was NASA's senior science representative in Australia, and from 1983 to 1987 he was director of space and life sciences at the JSC. He was in charge of the team that investigated the cause of death of the seven astronauts killed in the *Challenger* disaster. He left NASA in 1987 for the aerospace company Lockheed, where he managed several projects connected with the International Space Station. In 1997 he became president of Krug Life Sciences, an American company that provided medical services for the JSC. In 1998 Krug was bought by Wyle Laboratories, an American defense engineering company, and Kerwin became a senior vice president at Wyle. He retired in 2004.

JAMES LOVELL

(b. March 25, 1928, Cleveland, Ohio, U.S.)

James Arthur Lovell, Jr., was commander of the nearly disastrous Apollo 13 flight to the Moon in 1970. Lovell, a graduate (1952) of the U.S. Naval Academy, Annapolis, Md., became a test pilot and, at the time (1963) he was selected for the manned space program, was serving as a flight instructor and safety officer. He accompanied Frank Borman on the record-breaking 14-day flight of Gemini 7. Launched Dec. 4, 1965, Gemini 7 was joined in space by Gemini 6, launched 11 days later and manned by Walter M. Schirra, Jr., and Thomas P. Stafford, for the first successful space rendezvous. Lovell joined Edwin E. Aldrin for the last flight of the Gemini series, Gemini 12, which was launched on Nov. 11, 1966, and remained in orbit for four days.

Apollo 8 was launched on Dec. 21, 1968, and carried Lovell, Borman, and William Anders on the first manned flight around the Moon. This flight was the first of three preparatory to the Moon landing of Apollo 11.

With astronauts Fred W. Haise, John L. Swigert, Jr., and Lovell aboard, Apollo 13 lifted off on April 11, 1970, headed for the Fra Mauro Hills on the Moon. On April 13, approximately 205,000 miles (330,000 km) from Earth, an explosion ruptured an oxygen tank in the Service Module. The resulting shortage of power and oxygen forced the abandonment of the Moon mission. Apollo 13's crew changed course to swing once around the Moon and then return to Earth. With the successful return of Apollo 13 on April 17, Lovell had completed over 715 hours of space travel.

In 1971 Lovell became a deputy director of the Johnson Space Center, Houston, Texas. He retired from the navy and the space program in 1973 but remained in Houston as a corporation executive.

SHANNON LUCID
(b. Jan. 14, 1943, Shanghai, China)

From 1996 to 2007 Shannon Wells Lucid held the world record for most time in space by a woman, and from 1996 to 2002 she held the record for the longest-duration spaceflight by any U.S. astronaut.

Lucid was born in China as the daughter of Baptist missionaries and with her family spent several months in a Japanese prison camp near Shanghai during World War II. She received bachelor's, master's, and doctorate degrees from the University of Oklahoma; the Ph.D. was in biochemistry. She worked with the Oklahoma Medical Research Foundation in Oklahoma City until her 1978 selection as one of the first set of astronaut candidates to train for flights aboard the space shuttle.

Lucid first flew aboard the space shuttle in 1985 on a mission that deployed three communications satellites. She flew on three more space shuttle missions in 1989, 1991, and 1993, and then in 1996 rode the shuttle to the Russian space station Mir, where she spent 188 days, which was then a record for the longest-duration spaceflight by any U.S. astronaut. In all, Lucid spent a total of 223 days in space, then a record for most time in space by a woman.

In 2002 Lucid was named chief scientist of NASA, with responsibility for

Shannon Wells Lucid, exercising on a treadmill aboard the Russian space station Mir on March 28, 1996. NASA

overseeing the scientific quality of all NASA programs and for external communication of NASA's research objectives. She held that position until 2003, when she returned to NASA's Johnson Space Center in Houston.

CHRISTA MCAULIFFE

(b. Sept. 2, 1948, Boston, Mass., U.S.—d. Jan. 28, 1986, in-flight, off Cape Canaveral, Fla.)

Christa Corrigan McAuliffe was chosen to be the first teacher in space. The death of McAuliffe and her fellow crew members in the 1986 space shuttle *Challenger*

disaster was deeply felt by the nation and had a strong effect on the U.S. space program.

Christa Corrigan earned her B.A. from Framingham (Massachusetts) State College in 1970 and the same year married Steve McAuliffe. She received her M.A. in education from Bowie (Maryland) State College (now University) in 1978. In 1970 she began a teaching career that impressed both her colleagues and her students with her energy and dedication.

When in 1984 some 10,000 applications were processed to determine who would be the first teacher in space, McAuliffe was selected. In her

launch had been postponed for several days, and the night before the launch, central Florida was hit by a severe cold front that left ice on the launchpad. The shuttle finally was launched at 11:38 AM on Jan. 28, 1986. Just 73 seconds after liftoff the craft exploded, sending debris cascading into the Atlantic Ocean for more than an hour afterward. There were no survivors.

The live television coverage of the spectacular and tragic event, coupled with McAuliffe's winning, dynamic, and (not least) civilian presence onboard, halted shuttle missions for two and a half years, sorely damaged the reputation of NASA, and eroded public support for the space program.

Christa McAuliffe, 1985. NASA

application she proposed keeping a three-part journal of her experiences: the first part describing the training she would go through, the second chronicling the details of the actual flight, and the third relating her feelings and experiences back on Earth. She also planned to keep a video record of her activities. McAuliffe was to conduct at least two lessons while onboard the space shuttle to be simulcast to students around the world, and she was to spend the nine months following her return home lecturing to students across the United States.

Problems dogged the ill-fated *Challenger* mission from the start: the

BRUCE MCCANDLESS
(b. June 8, 1937, Boston, Mass., U.S.)

American naval aviator and astronaut Bruce McCandless II was the first person to conduct an untethered, free flight in space.

The son of an admiral and the grandson of a commodore, McCandless received a B.S. from the United States Naval Academy in Annapolis, Md., in 1958. After two years of flight training, he was designated a naval aviator in March 1960. McCandless then served as a fighter pilot and, briefly, as an instrument flight instructor in the U.S. Navy until 1964. He earned an M.S. in electrical engineering from Stanford University in Palo Alto, Calif., in 1965 and an M.B.A.

from the University of Houston at Clear Lake in 1987.

McCandless was among 19 astronaut candidates chosen by NASA in April 1966. He served as a member of the support crew for the Apollo 14 mission in 1971 and as the backup pilot for Skylab 2 in 1973. He also helped develop the Manned Maneuvering Unit (MMU), a rocket-propelled backpack that was worn by an astronaut during shuttle space walks.

McCandless's first spaceflight came as a mission specialist on STS-41-B aboard the *Challenger* space shuttle on Feb. 3, 1984. During this flight, McCandless tested the MMU in space walks and thus became the first person to fly in space without being tethered to a spacecraft. He traveled 300 feet (90 metres) away from the shuttle. Astronaut Robert Gibson's photograph of McCandless flying in space, with Earth in the background, became a symbol of the space program. The crew also deployed two communications satellites into orbit and returned to Earth on Feb. 11, 1984.

McCandless flew again as a mission specialist on STS-31, launching on the *Discovery* space shuttle on April 24, 1990. The STS-31 crew successfully deployed the Hubble Space Telescope into orbit. The shuttle landed at Edwards Air Force Base in California on April 29, 1990.

After leaving NASA, McCandless worked at Martin Marietta Corporation and was a senior research scientist at Lockheed Martin Space Systems in Littleton, Colo.

WILLIAM MCCOOL
(b. Sept. 23, 1961, San Diego, Calif., U.S.—d. Feb. 1, 2003, over Texas)

William Cameron McCool was pilot of the space shuttle *Columbia* on its final mission. McCool was educated at the U.S. Naval Academy; he earned a master's degree in computer science from the University of Maryland in 1985 and another in aeronautical engineering from the U.S. Naval Post-graduate School in 1992. He became a pilot for the U.S. Navy in 1986 and was chosen for the astronaut program in 1996.

JAMES MCDIVITT
(b. June 10, 1929, Chicago, Ill., U.S.)

James Alton McDivitt flew on two space flights. McDivitt joined the U.S. Air Force in 1951 and flew 145 combat missions in Korea. In 1959 he graduated first in his engineering class at the University of Michigan, Ann Arbor. He was an experimental test pilot at Edwards Air Force Base, Calif., when he was chosen as an astronaut in 1962.

McDivitt was the command pilot of Gemini 4 (launched June 3, 1965), a flight that included the first space walk by a

Astronaut Bruce McCandless floating in space on the first untethered space walk, Feb. 7, 1984. NASA

James A. McDivitt, 1971. NASA

U.S. astronaut, and was commander of Apollo 9 (launched March 3, 1969). He was then manager of the Apollo spacecraft program until he retired from the air force in 1972 with the rank of brigadier general and entered private business.

MICHAEL MELVILL
(b. Nov. 11, 1940?, Johannesburg, S.Af.)

Test pilot Michael Winston Melvill was the first commercial astronaut and the first person to travel into space aboard a privately funded spacecraft.

Melvill was raised in Durban, S.Af., and attended but did not graduate from Hilton College, a private boarding high school in Hilton. He immigrated to the United States with his family in 1967, becoming a U.S. citizen in 1972. He was hired by American aerospace engineer and aircraft designer Burt Rutan in 1978 and became Rutan's lead test pilot in 1982. Employed by Rutan's company, Scaled Composites in Mojave, Calif., from its inception in 1982, he served as the company's lead test pilot and later as its vice president and general manager.

On June 21, 2004, Melvill piloted SpaceShipOne on its first flight past the edge of space, becoming the first person to pilot a privately built aircraft into space and making history as the first commercial astronaut. Mechanical engine problems forced Melvill to cut the flight short and use a backup system to keep the aircraft under control. He received the first commercial astronaut wings from the Federal Aviation Administration after his flight. He returned to space aboard SpaceShipOne on Sept. 29, 2004, successfully completing the first of two flights into space that won Burt Rutan and SpaceShipOne the $10 million Ansari X Prize for the first private spacecraft that successfully completed two piloted flights with the equivalent weight of two passengers to the boundary of space in a two-week period.

Melvill continued working at Scaled Composites as vice president and general manager after his historic achievements. He holds nine aviation world records in speed and altitude.

EDGAR MITCHELL
(b. Sept. 17, 1930, Hereford, Texas, U.S.)

Edgar Dean Mitchell took part in the Apollo 14 mission (Jan. 31–Feb. 10, 1971), in which the uplands region north of the Fra Mauro crater on the Moon was explored by Mitchell and commander Alan B. Shepard, Jr.

Mitchell entered the U.S. Navy upon graduation from the Carnegie Institute of Technology, Pittsburgh, Pa. He was awarded an engineering degree by the Navy Postgraduate School, Monterey, Calif., in 1961 and a doctorate in aeronautics and astronautics by the Massachusetts Institute of Technology in 1964. He joined the manned space program in 1966.

He retired from the navy and the space program in 1972, and, interested in parapsychology, he founded the Institute of Noetic Sciences in Palo Alto, Calif.

BARBARA MORGAN
(b. Nov. 28, 1951, Fresno, Calif., U.S.)

Barbara Radding Morgan was the first teacher to travel into space. Morgan earned a B.A. in human biology from Stanford University in Palo Alto, Calif., in 1973. She received her teaching credentials from the College of Notre Dame (now Notre Dame de Namur University) in Belmont, Calif., in 1974, and taught remedial courses and elementary school on the Flathead Indian Reservation in Arlee, Mont., and in McCall, Idaho, between 1974 and 1978. After teaching

English and science in Quito, Ecua., for one year, Morgan returned to McCall, Idaho, where she taught second through fourth grades until 1998.

Morgan's astronaut career began on July 19, 1985, when she was selected as the backup candidate for NASA's Teacher in Space program. As the backup to American teacher Christa McAuliffe, Morgan attended training at NASA's Johnson Space Center in Houston from September 1985 to January 1986. When McAuliffe perished in the *Challenger* disaster, Morgan replaced her as the Teacher in Space designee and continued to work with NASA's education division.

Morgan was selected as a mission specialist in 1998 and underwent two years of training and evaluation at the Johnson Space Center. In 2002 she was assigned as a mission specialist to the crew of STS-118, which was originally scheduled for launch in November 2003 but was delayed for several years after the *Columbia* disaster on Feb. 1, 2003. Morgan finally flew into space on the space shuttle *Endeavour* on Aug. 8, 2007, on STS-118. The mission was an assembly-and-repair trip to the International Space Station (ISS). Morgan operated the shuttle's and station's robotic arms to install hardware on the ISS and to support space walks. In addition, schoolchildren enjoyed the lessons she conducted while in space. STS-118 returned to Earth on Aug. 21, 2007.

Even though Morgan did not participate in the Educator Astronaut Project (the successor to the Teacher in Space program) and flew on STS-118 as a standard mission specialist, NASA often referred to her as an "educator astronaut" and a "mission specialist educator" in its press releases and media briefings. Hence, she is widely considered to be NASA's first educator astronaut.

Morgan left NASA in 2008 to join Boise State University in Idaho as the distinguished educator in residence, a faculty position created specifically for her that entailed a dual appointment to the colleges of engineering and education.

STORY MUSGRAVE

(b. Aug. 19, 1935, Boston, Mass., U.S.)

Franklin Story Musgrave made six flights into space. After serving in the Marine Corps, Musgrave earned an impressive list of academic credentials, including bachelor's or master's degrees in mathematics, operations analysis, chemistry, literature, and physiology, as well as a medical degree from Columbia University (1964).

In 1967, as an expert on cardiovascular and exercise physiology, he was picked by NASA as one of a group of scientist-astronauts to serve on future space missions. While training as a jet pilot, he began designing space suits, life-support systems, and other equipment used for extravehicular activity (i.e., space walks) on NASA missions, a field in which he eventually became preeminent.

Musgrave's first space mission was on STS-6, the maiden flight of the *Challenger* space shuttle, in April 1983. He then

Story Musgrave, 1971. NASA

served as flight engineer on the crew of Spacelab-2 in July 1985, a mission that performed astronomical research. He was a mission specialist on STS-33 (November 1989), STS-44 (November 1991), and STS-80 (November–December 1996).

His most important mission came in December 1993, when, as payload commander on STS-61, he led the crew in a successful effort to repair the faultily constructed Hubble Space Telescope. Musgrave also served as capsule communicator (i.e., the ground-based communicator with crews in space) for many Skylab and space shuttle missions, and he published many scientific papers on aerospace medicine, exercise physiology, and other subjects.

BILL NELSON
(b. Sept. 29, 1942, Miami, Fla., U.S.)

American politician Clarence William "Bill" Nelson was the second sitting member of Congress to travel into space. Nelson earned a B.A. in political science from Yale University in 1965 and received a doctorate of law (J.D.) from the University of Virginia School of Law in 1968. He was admitted to the Florida bar the same year. He served in the U.S. Army Reserve for six years (1965–71), saw active duty for two years (1968–70), and earned the rank of captain.

After starting his law practice in Melbourne, Fla., in 1970 and working as a legislative assistant to Gov. Reubin Askew in 1971, Nelson launched his own political career and was elected to the Florida House of Representatives in 1972. He served in the state legislature from 1972 to 1979. He was elected as a Democrat to the U.S. House of Representatives, and he served six terms (1979–91) as a representative for Florida's 9th and 11th congressional districts.

Nelson, who was chair of the House space subcommittee, began his astronaut training at the Johnson Space Center in Houston in September 1985. On Jan. 12, 1986, he flew aboard the *Columbia* space shuttle as a payload specialist on the STS-61-C mission. During the six-day flight, the seven-man crew launched a communications satellite and performed several experiments in materials processing and astrophysics, including an infrared imaging experiment and a handheld protein crystal growth experiment. STS-61-C returned to Earth on Jan. 18, 1986.

Nelson was a candidate for governor of Florida in 1990, but he lost in the Democratic Party primaries. In 1994 he was elected to the Florida cabinet as treasurer, insurance commissioner, and fire marshal. He served there until his election to the U.S. Senate in November 2000. He was reelected in 2006.

ELLEN OCHOA
(b. May 10, 1958, Los Angeles, Calif., U.S.)

Ellen Ochoa was the first Hispanic female astronaut. Ochoa studied electrical

The first Hispanic female astronaut, Ellen Ochoa, was part of the space shuttle Discovery *mission that marked the first docking to the International Space Station.* NASA

engineering at Stanford University, earning a master's degree (1981) and a doctorate (1985). A specialist in the development of optical systems, she worked as a research engineer at Sandia National Laboratories and at the Ames Research Center of NASA. She helped create several systems and methods that were awarded patents, including optical systems for the detection of imperfections in a repeating pattern and for the recognition of objects.

In 1990 Ochoa was selected by NASA to participate in its astronaut program, and she completed her training in 1991. In April 1993 she served as mission specialist aboard the shuttle *Discovery*, becoming the first Hispanic woman to travel into space. She was part of the *Atlantis* mission in November 1994, and in 1999 she was a member of the *Discovery* crew that executed the first docking to the International Space Station (ISS). Ochoa returned to the ISS in 2002.

SALLY RIDE

(b. May 26, 1951, Encino, Calif., U.S.)

Sally Kristen Ride was the first American woman to travel into outer space. Only two other women preceded her: Valentina Tereshkova (1963) and Svetlana Savitskaya (1982), both from the former Soviet Union.

Ride showed great early promise as a tennis player, but she eventually gave up her plans to play professionally and

Sally Ride serving as mission specialist on the flight deck of the space shuttle orbiter Challenger. NASA

attended Stanford University, where she earned bachelor's degrees in English and physics (1973). In 1978, as a doctoral candidate and teaching assistant in laser physics at Stanford, she was selected by NASA as one of six women astronaut candidates. She received a Ph.D. in astrophysics and began her training and evaluation courses that same year. In August 1979 she completed her NASA training, obtained a pilot's license, and became eligible for assignment as a U.S. space shuttle mission specialist.

On June 18, 1983, she became the first American woman in space while rocketing into orbit aboard the shuttle orbiter *Challenger*. The shuttle mission lasted six days, during which time she helped deploy two communications satellites and carry out a variety of experiments. She served on a second space mission aboard *Challenger* in October 1984; the crew included another woman, Ride's childhood friend Kathryn Sullivan, who became the first American woman to walk in space.

Ride was training for a third shuttle mission when the *Challenger* exploded after launch in January 1986, a catastrophe that caused NASA to suspend shuttle flights for more than two years. Ride served on the presidential commission appointed to investigate the accident, and she repeated that role as a member of the commission that investigated the in-flight breakup of the orbiter *Columbia* in February 2003.

Ride married fellow astronaut Steven Hawley in 1982; they divorced five years later. Ride resigned from NASA in 1987, and in 1989 she became a professor of physics at the University of California, San Diego, and director of its California Space Institute (until 1996). In 1999–2000 she held executive positions with Space. com, a Web site presenting space, astronomy, and technology content.

From the 1990s Ride initiated or headed a number of programs and organizations devoted to fostering science in education, particularly to providing support for schoolgirls interested in science, mathematics, or technology. She also wrote or collaborated on several children's books about space exploration and her personal experiences as an astronaut.

STUART ROOSA
(b. Aug. 16, 1933, Durango, Colo., U.S.—d. Dec. 12, 1994, Falls Church, Va.)

Stuart Allen Roosa participated in the Apollo 14 mission (Jan. 31–Feb. 9, 1971), in which the uplands region of the Moon, 15 miles (24 km) north of the Fra Mauro crater, was explored. While he orbited overhead in the Command Module, commander Alan B. Shepard and Edgar D. Mitchell landed on the Moon.

After spending two years at Oklahoma A & M College, Stillwater, Roosa joined the U.S. Air Force in 1953. Two years later he resumed his studies at the University of Colorado, Boulder, which awarded him a B.S. degree in aeronautical engineering. He piloted both standard and experimental aircraft before becoming an astronaut in 1966. After 1976, when Roosa left the space program, he held a series of executive positions in private businesses in Greece and the United States.

JERRY ROSS
(b. Jan. 20, 1948, Crown Point, Ind., U.S.)

Jerry Lynn Ross was the first person to be launched into space seven times. Ross earned a B.S. in mechanical engineering in 1970 at Purdue University in West Lafayette, Ind. After receiving a master's degree in mechanical engineering in 1972, he started active duty with the U.S. Air Force (USAF). He graduated from the flight test engineer course at the USAF Test Pilot School in 1976. During his career Ross flew more than 20 different types of aircraft, mainly military aircraft, and clocked more than 4,000 flying hours.

In February 1979 he was assigned to NASA's Johnson Space Center (JSC) in Houston. In May 1980, while working there as a payload officer and a flight controller, he was selected to be an astronaut. Since then he has logged more than 58 days in space, including more than 58 hours on nine space walks. His space missions included flying as the mission specialist on seven flights: STS-61-B (1985, deployment of three communications satellites), STS-27 (1988, deployment of a military reconnaissance satellite), STS-37 (1991, launch of the Compton Gamma Ray Observatory), STS-55 (1993, payload of the German Spacelab D-2), STS-74 (1995, the second docking of a space shuttle with the Russian Mir space station), STS-88 (1998, the first assembly mission for the International Space Station [ISS]), and STS-110 (2002, another ISS assembly mission).

Ross held many positions with NASA, including branch chief of the Astronaut Office at the Kennedy Space Center and chief astronaut for the Engineering and Safety Center. He retired from the air force as a colonel in 2000. In 2007 Ross became chief of the Vehicle Integration Test Office at the JSC.

WALTER SCHIRRA
(b. March 12, 1923, Hackensack, N.J., —d. May 3, 2007, La Jolla, Calif.)

Walter Marty Schirra, Jr., manned the Mercury *Sigma 7* (1962) and was command pilot of Gemini 6 (1965), which made the first rendezvous in space. He was the only astronaut to fly in the Mercury, Gemini, and Apollo space programs.

Walter M. Schirra, Jr., 1962. NASA/Johnson Space Center

Schirra began flying at 13 and became a naval aviator after graduating from the U.S. Naval Academy, Annapolis, Md., in 1945. He flew 90 missions in the Korean War. A test pilot, he was one of the original seven astronauts named in 1959. On Oct. 3, 1962, Schirra orbited Earth six times in *Sigma 7*. His scheduled flight with Thomas P. Stafford in Gemini 6 was postponed twice because of technical problems. Gemini 6 was finally launched on Dec. 15, 1965, 11 days after Gemini 7. Schirra successfully rendezvoused with Gemini 7, maneuvering to within one foot of the craft.

Schirra commanded the Apollo 7 flight (Oct. 11–22, 1968), accompanied by Donn Eisele and R. Walter Cunningham, on the first manned Apollo mission. They tested the guidance and control systems and the restarting capability of the rocket engines for future lunar flights.

After retiring from the navy and the space program in 1969, Schirra held executive positions in private firms in Colorado. In 2000 he was inducted into the Naval Aviation Hall of Honor.

HARRISON SCHMITT
(b. July 3, 1935, Santa Rita, N.M., U.S.)

Geologist, astronaut, and politician Harrison Hagan "Jack" Schmitt was one of the last two men on the Moon.

Apollo 17 *geologist-astronaut Harrison Schmitt at the foot of a huge split boulder, Dec. 13, 1972, during the mission's third extravehicular exploration of the Taurus-Littrow Valley landing site.* NASA

Schmitt was educated at the California Institute of Technology (Caltech) in Pasadena, the University of Oslo, and Harvard University in Cambridge, Mass., where he received a Ph.D. in geology in 1964. He was employed by the U.S. Geological Survey in its astrogeology branch at Flagstaff, Ariz. (1964–65), before joining NASA. He participated in the lunar landing of Apollo 17 in December 1972. Schmitt and commander Eugene A. Cernan were the last men on the Moon, spending 22 hours and 5 minutes on the lunar surface and traveling 36 km (22 miles). Schmitt was elected to the U.S. Senate from New Mexico in 1976 but was defeated in a bid for a second term in 1982. In 1994 he became an adjunct professor of engineering at the University of Wisconsin in Madison.

DAVID SCOTT

(b. June 6, 1932, San Antonio, Texas, U.S.)

After graduation from the U.S. Military Academy at West Point in 1954, Scott transferred to the U.S. Air Force and took flight training. He earned an M.S. in aeronautics and astronautics from the Massachusetts Institute of Technology and went to Edwards Air Force Base in California to train as a test pilot. In 1963 he was among the third group of U.S. astronauts chosen.

Scott and commander Neil Armstrong manned the flight of Gemini 8 (March 16, 1966). They successfully rendezvoused and docked with an unmanned Agena target vehicle, but an electrical failure caused the Agena-Gemini craft to tumble wildly. The Gemini capsule was separated from the Agena. Control was finally reestablished, but the mission had to be aborted. Scott and Armstrong landed 10 hours 42 minutes after takeoff.

Scott served as command module pilot of the Apollo 9 flight with commander James McDivitt and lunar module pilot Russell Schweickart; their mission was launched on March 3, 1969. In Earth orbit these men rendezvoused and docked the Command Module with the Lunar Module, which was on its first manned flight, and they successfully tested all systems necessary for a lunar landing.

On July 26, 1971, Scott, lunar module pilot James Irwin, and command module pilot Alfred Worden were launched on the Apollo 15 flight. After a 3 ½-day trip Scott and Irwin landed on the Moon, at the base of the Apennine Mountains near a gorge called Hadley Rille. Using the Lunar Roving Vehicle, they covered about 28 km (18 miles) on three separate treks and spent more than 17 hours outside their Lunar Module. The mission returned to Earth on August 7.

From 1972 to 1975 Scott was a member of the administrative staff of the Apollo-Soyuz Test Project. He then became director of the Dryden Flight Research Center at Edwards Air Force Base. He left the space program in 1977 to enter private business in Los Angeles. In 2004 he wrote a book, *Two Sides of the Moon: Our Story of the Cold War Space Race*, with Soviet cosmonaut Aleksey Leonov.

ALAN SHEPARD

(b. Nov. 18, 1923, East Derry, N.H., U.S.—d. July 21, 1998, Monterey, Calif.)

Alan Bartlett Shepard, Jr., was the first American astronaut to travel in space.

Shepard graduated from the U.S. Naval Academy, Annapolis, Md., in 1944 and served in the Pacific during World War II. He became a naval test pilot, and in 1958 he graduated from the Naval War College, Newport, R.I. In 1959 he became one of the original seven astronauts chosen for the U.S. Mercury program by NASA.

On May 5, 1961, Shepard made a 15-minute suborbital flight in the *Freedom 7* spacecraft, which reached an altitude of 115 miles (185 km). The flight came 23 days after Major Yury Gagarin of the Soviet Union became the first man to orbit Earth.

Shepard commanded the Apollo 14 flight (Jan. 31–Feb. 9, 1971; with Stuart A. Roosa and Edgar D. Mitchell), which involved the first landing in the lunar highlands. Shepard headed NASA's astronaut office from 1963 to 1969 and then from 1971 to 1974, when he retired from the navy and the space program to undertake a career in private business in Texas.

Alan B. Shepard, Jr., 1970. NASA/Johnson Space Center

Alan Shepard's 15 minutes of fame came in 1961. About three weeks after Yury Gagarin made his groundbreaking flight, Shepard made a quarter-hour suborbital flight, making him the first American in space. NASA

DONALD SLAYTON

(b. March 1, 1924, Sparta, Wis., U.S.—d. June 13, 1993, League City, Texas)

Donald Kent "Deke" Slayton was one of the original seven Project Mercury astronauts in 1959 but did not make a space flight until 1975.

Slayton joined the U.S. Air Force in 1942 and flew 56 combat missions during World War II. After the war he earned a B.S. in aeronautical engineering (1949) from the University of Minnesota and then became an engineer with the Boeing Aircraft Company. In 1951 he was recalled to active duty with the Minnesota Air National Guard, and in 1955 he became a test pilot at Edwards Air Force Base in California.

After joining the Mercury astronaut program, Slayton was grounded because he was found to have an irregular heartbeat. He proved instrumental, however, as the director of flight crew operations at the Johnson Space Center, where he directed astronaut training and chose crews for nearly all the Gemini and Apollo missions.

In 1975, after his heart ailment unaccountably disappeared, Slayton at age 51 was named docking module pilot for the Apollo-Soyuz mission (July 15–24, 1975; with Thomas P. Stafford and Vance D. Brand). After that flight was completed, Slayton served as manager of the orbital flight tests of the space shuttle until he retired in 1982. He then founded and directed Space Services, Inc., a pioneering company that launched small satellites.

THOMAS STAFFORD

(b. Sept. 17, 1930, Weatherford, Okla., U.S.)

Thomas Patten Stafford flew two Gemini rendezvous missions (1965–66) and commanded the Apollo 10 mission (1969)—the final test of Apollo systems before the first manned landing on the Moon—as well as the Apollo spacecraft that docked with a Soviet Soyuz craft in space in 1975.

A graduate (1952) of the U.S. Naval Academy, Annapolis, Md., Stafford transferred to the air force and studied at the Air Force Experimental Flight Test School. Stafford was Walter M. Schirra's copilot on the Gemini 6 mission, launched Dec. 15, 1965. Their rendezvous with the previously launched Gemini 7 was the world's first successful space rendezvous. On June 3, 1966, Eugene A. Cernan and command pilot Stafford were launched into space in Gemini 9. Stafford performed three rendezvous with a target vehicle, but a protective covering on the target had failed to detach, preventing docking.

Apollo 10, manned by Stafford, Cernan, and John W. Young, was launched on May 18, 1969. Three days later the spacecraft attained lunar orbit. The flight rehearsed every phase of a Moon landing except the landing itself. Cernan and Stafford descended in the Lunar Module to within 9.5 miles (15 km) of the

Moon's surface. Apollo 10 completed 31 orbits of the Moon before returning to Earth, landing in the Pacific Ocean on May 26.

Stafford resigned from the space program in 1975 to become commander of the Air Force Flight Test Center, Edwards Air Force Base, Calif. In 1978 he was promoted to lieutenant general and became Air Force Deputy Chief of Staff for Research and Development, stationed in Washington, D.C. After retiring from the air force in 1979, he became an executive of a transportation company in Oklahoma.

JACK SWIGERT
(b. Aug. 30, 1931, Denver, Colo., U.S.—d. Dec. 27, 1982, Washington, D.C.)

John "Jack" Leonard Swigert, Jr., was a participant in the Apollo 13 mission (April 11–17, 1970), in which an intended Moon landing was canceled because of a ruptured fuel-cell oxygen tank in the Service Module. The crew, consisting of Swigert, Fred W. Haise, Jr., and commander James A. Lovell, Jr., returned safely to Earth, making use of the life-support system in the Lunar Module. Swigert was a last-minute substitute for Thomas K. Mattingly, who was ill.

Swigert graduated from the University of Colorado, Boulder, in 1953 and was awarded a master's degree by the Rensselaer Polytechnic Institute, Troy, N.Y., in 1965. Before becoming an astronaut in 1966, he was a U.S. Air Force pilot

in Japan and Korea and a commercial test pilot.

Swigert took a leave of absence from the space program in 1973 to become executive director of the Committee on Science and Technology of the U.S. House of Representatives. He resigned from the committee and from NASA in 1977 and entered private business in Virginia. He ran unsuccessfully for a seat in the U.S. Senate in 1978 but was elected from Colorado to the House of Representatives in 1982, shortly before his death.

DAVID WALKER
(b. May 20, 1944, Columbus, Ga., U.S.—d. April 23, 2001, Houston, Texas)

David Mathieson Walker was the pilot of the space shuttle *Discovery* in 1984 and the commander of three later space shuttle missions. After graduating from the U.S. Naval Academy, Annapolis, Md., in 1966, Walker became one of the navy's "top gun" fighter pilots; he earned six Navy Air Medals for combat duty during the Vietnam War. NASA selected him to become an astronaut in 1978. As pilot of the *Discovery* shuttle, he played an integral part in the first space salvage mission in history; the crew successfully retrieved two communications satellites that had been stranded in the wrong orbits. Walker later served as mission commander of the *Atlantis* shuttle in 1989, *Discovery* in 1992, and *Endeavour* in 1995.

EDWARD WHITE

(b. Nov. 14, 1930, San Antonio, Texas, U.S.—d. Jan. 27, 1967, Cape Kennedy, Fla.)

Edward Higgins White II was the first U.S. astronaut to walk in space. White graduated from the U.S. Military Academy, West Point, N.Y., in 1952 and was commissioned a second lieutenant in the U.S. Air Force. He took flight training and served in a fighter squadron in Germany. In 1959 he received his M.S. in aeronautical engineering from the University of Michigan, Ann Arbor, and graduated from the Air Force Test Pilot School, Edwards Air Force Base, California.

White was selected in 1962 as a member of the second group of astronauts. Often called the most physically fit astronaut, he was chosen to join James A. McDivitt on the four-day orbital flight of Gemini 4, launched on June 3, 1965. During the third orbit White emerged from the spacecraft, floated in space for about 20 minutes, and became the first person to propel himself in space with a maneuvering unit. White was subsequently one of the three-man crew of Apollo 1 who in 1967 were the first casualties of the U.S. space program, killed during a flight simulation (the others were Virgil I. Grissom and Roger B. Chaffee).

PEGGY WHITSON

(b. Feb. 9, 1960, Mount Ayr, Iowa, U.S.)

Biochemist and astronaut Peggy Annette Whitson was the first female commander of the International Space Station (ISS) and is the American astronaut and woman who has spent the most time in space.

Whitson received a B.S. in biology and chemistry from Iowa Wesleyan College in Mount Pleasant, Iowa, in 1981 and a doctorate in biochemistry from Rice University in Houston in 1985. In 1986 she moved to NASA's Johnson Space Center (JSC) in Houston as a research associate. She later worked as the supervisor for the Biochemistry Research Group at KRUG International, a NASA medical sciences contractor at the JSC.

Whitson had a long and varied career at NASA before her selection as an astronaut candidate. Among other positions, she worked in the Biomedical Operations and Research branch at the JSC from 1989 to 1993 and was the deputy division chief of the Medical Sciences division at the JSC from 1993 to 1996. She also participated in joint efforts between American and Soviet (later Russian) scientists.

Whitson began her astronaut training in August 1996. After completing two years of training, she worked in various

Gemini 4 astronaut Edward White during his historic 21-minute space walk on June 3, 1965. White was secured to the Gemini spacecraft by a 7.6-metre (25-foot) umbilical and tether line. He used a self-maneuvering unit to facilitate movement outside the craft. NASA

technical positions at the Operations Planning branch of NASA's Astronaut Office. She flew into space for the first time on June 5, 2002, as a flight engineer on Expedition 5 to the ISS aboard the space shuttle *Endeavour* on mission STS-111. On board the ISS, she conducted more than 20 experiments in microgravity and human life sciences and also operated and installed commercial payloads and hardware systems. She was designated as the first NASA ISS science officer and also performed a space walk to install shielding on a service module and to deploy a science payload. After nearly 185 days in space, she returned to Earth aboard STS-113, landing on December 7.

Whitson traveled into space for a second time on Oct. 10, 2007, aboard Soyuz TMA-11 with Yury Malenchenko of Russia and Sheikh Muszaphar Shukor of Malaysia as the commander of the Expedition 16 mission, becoming the first female commander of the ISS. As commander, Whitson supervised and directed a significant expansion of the living and working space on the ISS, including the installation of components made by European, Japanese, and Canadian space agencies. She also performed five space walks during the six-month mission to carry out maintenance and assembly tasks.

After spending nearly 192 days in space, Whitson returned to Earth aboard Soyuz TMA-11 on April 19, 2008. The crew of Soyuz TMA-11 had a difficult and dangerous ride back to Earth; the Soyuz's equipment module failed to separate properly from the reentry module, and so the craft followed an unusually steep descent trajectory. The crew made an extremely hard landing, which missed the target by 470 km (300 miles). Whitson suffered no permanent injuries.

Whitson spent nearly 377 days in space during her two long-duration tours of duty to the ISS, which made her NASA's most experienced astronaut. Her total of six career space walks and their combined duration of 39 hours 46 minutes were also records for a female astronaut. After her second space mission, Whitson returned to NASA as an active astronaut.

SUNITA WILLIAMS
(b. Sept. 19, 1965, Euclid, Ohio, U.S.)

Sunita Williams holds the record for longest spaceflight by a woman. In 1983 Williams entered the U.S. Naval Academy at Annapolis, Md. She was made an ensign in 1987 and reported for aviator training at the Naval Aviation Training Command. In July 1989 she began combat helicopter training. She flew in helicopter support squadrons during the preparations for the Persian Gulf War and the establishment of no-fly zones over Kurdish areas of Iraq, as well as in relief missions during Hurricane Andrew in 1992 in Miami.

In 1993 she became a naval test pilot and later a test pilot instructor, flying more than 30 different aircraft and logging

The space-longevity record for a woman goes to astronaut Sunita Williams. For 195 days, Williams worked and lived aboard the International Space Station, beginning Dec. 9, 2006. Pal Pillai/AFP/ Getty Images

more than 2,770 flight hours. When selected for the astronaut program, she was stationed aboard the USS *Saipan*.

Williams completed an M.S. in engineering management from the Florida Institute of Technology in Melbourne in 1995, and she entered astronaut training in 1998. She traveled to Moscow, where she received training in robotics and other International Space Station (ISS) operational technologies while working with the Russian Federal Space Agency and with crews preparing for expeditions to the ISS.

On Dec. 9, 2006, Williams flew aboard the space shuttle *Discovery* on the STS-116 mission to the ISS, where she was a flight engineer for Expeditions 14 and 15. During her stay at the space station, she made four space walks totaling more than 29 hours outside the spacecraft and spent a total of more than 195 days in space, both of which were records for women in space. Williams landed at Edwards Air Force Base in California with the crew of STS-117 on June 22, 2007.

ALFRED WORDEN

(b. Feb. 7, 1932, Jackson, Mich., U.S.)

Alfred Worden graduated in 1955 from the U.S. Military Academy at West Point, N.Y., and he earned M.S. degrees in astronautical and aeronautical engineering and in instrumentation engineering from the University of Michigan, Ann Arbor, in 1963. He was a U.S. Air Force pilot and a commercial test pilot before joining the space program in 1966.

During the Apollo 15 mission, he orbited the Moon while commander David Scott and lunar module pilot James Irwin descended to the Moon's surface. On the return trip, Worden took a space walk—at what was then the record distance from Earth for such activity, about 315,000 km (196,000 miles)—retrieving cassettes containing films of the Moon from the rear of a subsatellite that they had sent into orbit two days previously.

After serving at NASA's Ames Research Center in Moffett Field, Calif., from 1972 to 1975, Worden resigned from the air force and the space program to enter private enterprises in Colorado and Florida. He wrote a book of poetry, *Hello Earth—Greetings from* Endeavour (1974), and a children's book, *I Want to Know About a Flight to the Moon* (1974).

JOHN YOUNG

(b. Sept. 24, 1930, San Francisco, Calif., U.S.)

John Watts Young was an American astronaut who participated in the Gemini, Apollo, and space shuttle projects. He served as Virgil I. Grissom's copilot on Gemini 3 (1965), the first U.S. two-man space flight.

After graduating from Georgia Institute of Technology (1952) with a degree in aeronautical engineering, Young joined the U.S. Navy. He served in Korea before participating in a test project, during which, in 1962, he set two altitude records in an F4B Navy jet. During 1962–64 Young trained for his part in NASA projects.

Gemini 3, launched on March 23, 1965, reached a maximum altitude of 139 miles (224 km) on the initial orbit. The orbit was changed three times, and after 4 hours 53 minutes flight time, the spacecraft landed in the South Atlantic Ocean.

John W. Young. NASA/Johnson Space Center

After this flight U.S. Pres. Lyndon B. Johnson conferred the NASA Exceptional Service medal on Young.

On July 18, 1966, Young joined Michael Collins on the Gemini 10 flight. The two docked with an Agena target vehicle and, using the Agena's engine, attained an altitude of 475 miles (764 km). On May 18, 1969, Apollo 10 was launched, with Thomas P. Stafford, Eugene A. Cernan, and Young on board. The flight, which orbited the Moon, was the last checkout of Apollo systems before the Moon landing of Apollo 11.

Young was commander of the Apollo 16 mission (April 16–27, 1972; with Charles M. Duke, Jr., and Thomas K. Mattingly), the fifth manned landing on the Moon. He retired from the navy in 1976 but remained with the space program, becoming chief of the astronaut office. He was commander of the first space shuttle mission (April 12–14, 1981; with Robert L. Crippen), guiding the orbiter *Columbia* to a landing at Edwards Air Force Base in California after it had circled the Earth 36 times.

In 1983 Young commanded the joint NASA and European Space Agency (ESA) mission, which from November 28 to December 8 carried Spacelab, a scientific workshop, in the orbiter *Columbia*'s payload bay.

CHAPTER 9

SOVIET AND RUSSIAN COSMONAUTS

Spurred by competition from the United States, the former Soviet Union developed its own space program, out of which emerged a daring group of men and women known as cosmonauts. Like their U.S. counterparts of the day, early Soviet cosmonauts came up through the ranks of the military to earn their spot in the space program. For their bravery and service they were awarded the country's greatest honour, being named a Hero of the Soviet Union. Today's cosmonauts are graduates of the Yury Gagarin Cosmonaut Training Centre, named for the first man in space.

The lives of past and present cosmonauts—before, during, and after their time in the Soviet/Russian space program—offer an intriguing study of how space exploration can change and enrich a person's life.

PAVEL BELYAYEV
(b. June 26, 1925, Chelishchevo, Russia, U.S.S.R. [now Russia]—d. Jan. 10, 1970, Moscow)

Pavel Ivanovich Belyayev served as the pilot of the Voskhod 2 spacecraft during the Soviet Union's eighth manned space mission, launched March 18, 1965, the flight on which Aleksey Leonov, Belyayev's copilot, became the first man to walk in space.

Belyayev began training as a fighter pilot in 1943 and saw combat against the Japanese late in World War II. After the war he remained in naval aviation. While attending the Soviet Air Force Academy, Moscow, in late 1959, he was selected for training as one of the original group of cosmonauts. For his part in the Voskhod 2 flight, he was proclaimed a Hero of the Soviet Union.

VALERY BYKOVSKY
(b. Aug. 2, 1934, Pavlovsky Posad, Russia, U.S.S.R. [now Russia])

Valery Fyodorovich Bykovsky orbited Earth 81 times in the spacecraft Vostok 5, from June 14 to 19, 1963. Bykovsky started flying lessons at the age of 16, joined the army in 1952, and in 1959 became a jet fighter pilot. In the early 1960s he was trained as a cosmonaut at the Zhukovsky Military Engineering Academy.

On June 16, 1963, after Bykovsky had been in orbit two days, the Soviet Union launched Vostok 6, carrying Valentina Tereshkova, the first woman to travel in space. The two ships held parallel orbits, at one point approaching to within 3 miles (5 km) of one another, but did not rendezvous. They returned to Earth three hours apart.

Bykovsky was made a member of the Communist Party on June 18, while still in orbit, and after his return he received his country's highest honour, Hero of the Soviet Union. He was one of the few men to receive the Soviet Union's highest

combat award during peacetime, the Order of the Red Star, presumably for air-combat action in a border incident.

He was chief of cosmonaut training for the Apollo-Soyuz Test Project, which was carried out in July 1975, and was command pilot of Soyuz 22, a 190-hour flight that began on Sept. 15, 1976. On Aug. 26, 1978, Bykovsky lifted off with East German cosmonaut Sigmund Jähn aboard Soyuz 31. On the space station Salyut 6, Bykovsky and Jähn conducted scientific experiments before returning to Earth on Soyuz 29 on Sept. 3, 1978.

GEORGY DOBROVOLSKY
(b. June 1, 1928, Odessa, Ukraine, U.S.S.R. [now Ukraine]—d. June 29, 1971, in space)

Georgy Timofeyevich Dobrovolsky was mission commander on the Soyuz 11 mission in which he, along with design engineer Viktor Ivanovich Patsayev and flight engineer Vladislav Nikolayevich Volkov, remained in space a record 24 days. They created the first manned orbital scientific station by docking their Soyuz 11 spacecraft with the unmanned Salyut station launched two months earlier. While in the space station, they performed meteorologic and plant-growing experiments.

Dobrovolsky and the other two cosmonauts were found dead in their space capsule after it made a perfect landing in Kazakhstan. Death was caused by decompression resulting from a leak in their capsule when a hatch was improperly closed.

KONSTANTIN FEOKTISTOV

(b. Feb. 7, 1926, Voronezh, Russia,
U.S.S.R. [now Russia])

Russian spacecraft designer and cosmonaut Konstantin Petrovich Feoktistov took part, with Vladimir M. Komarov and Boris B. Yegorov, in the world's first multi-manned spaceflight, Voskhod 1 (1964).

When Voronezh was occupied in World War II, Feoktistov, who was then only 16, worked as a scout for the Soviet army. He was captured by the Germans and sentenced to death by firing squad. Shot through the neck, he feigned death and escaped from a burial trench.

He later attended Moscow N.E. Bauman Higher Technical School and worked for a time as a factory engineer. In 1955 he earned the equivalent of a Ph.D. and from that time worked in the Soviet space program designing spacecraft and equipment. Feoktistov was awarded the Order of the Red Banner of Labour after the launching of the first artificial satellite, Sputnik 1 (Oct. 4, 1957), and again after the first successful manned flight by Yury Gagarin (April 12, 1961).

During the flight of Voskhod 1, Oct. 12– 13, 1964, Feoktistov carried out extensive scientific experiments and observations beyond the capability of previous cosmonauts. In addition to being the first craft to carry more than one man, Voskhod 1 was the first to carry specialists (a doctor and an engineer) and the first to make a soft landing on the ground. After the Voskhod 1 flight, Feoktistov returned to engineering and played a major role in designing the Salyut space stations.

YURY GAGARIN

(b. March 9, 1934, near Gzhatsk, Russian
S.F.S.R. [now Gagarin, Russia]—d.
March 27, 1968, near Moscow, U.S.S.R.
[now Russia])

In 1961 Soviet cosmonaut Yury Alekseyevich Gagarin became the first man to travel into space.

The son of a carpenter on a collective farm, Gagarin graduated as a molder from a trade school near Moscow in 1951. He continued his studies at the industrial college at Saratov and concurrently took a course in flying. On completing this course, he entered the Soviet Air Force cadet school at Orenburg, from which he graduated in 1957.

Gagarin's four and three-quarter-ton Vostok 1 spacecraft was launched at 9:07 AM Moscow time on April 12, 1961, orbited Earth once in 1 hour 29 minutes at a maximum altitude of 187 miles (301 km), and landed at 10:55 AM in the Soviet Union. His spaceflight brought him immediate worldwide fame; he was awarded the Order of Lenin and given the headtitles of Hero of the Soviet Union and Pilot Cosmonaut of the Soviet Union. Monuments were raised to him and

The former Soviet Union edged the United States in the space race when it launched Yury Gagarin into orbit in 1961. AFP/ Getty Images

and from 1962 he served as a deputy to the Supreme Soviet. Gagarin was killed with another pilot in the crash of a two-seat jet aircraft while on what was described as a routine training flight. His ashes were placed in a niche in the Kremlin wall. After his death in 1968 the town of Gzhatsk was renamed Gagarin.

PYOTR KLIMUK

(b. July 10, 1942, Komarovka, Belorussia, U.S.S.R. [now Belarus])

Pyotr Ilyich Klimuk flew three times in space and was head of the Yury Gagarin Cosmonaut Training Centre near Moscow.

Klimuk became a cosmonaut trainee in 1965, at age 23. Between 1967 and 1969 he trained for a flight around the Moon that was eventually canceled. He flew his first mission into space in 1973 as commander of Soyuz 13, during which he and his crewmate Valentin Lebedev spent a week in Earth orbit.

Having transferred into space station training, Klimuk flew his second spaceflight in 1975 as commander of Soyuz 18,

streets renamed in his honour across the Soviet Union.

Gagarin never went into space again but took an active part in training other cosmonauts. He made several tours to other nations following his historic flight,

a 63-day flight to the Salyut 4 space station. At the time, this was the longest Soviet spaceflight. He ended his career with a third mission in 1978, as commander of Soyuz 30, during which a Polish cosmonaut, Mirosław Hermaszewski, accompanied him on a short visit to the Salyut 6 space station.

Klimuk officially resigned as a cosmonaut in 1982. From 1982 to 1991 he headed the political department at the Yury Gagarin Cosmonaut Training Centre. After the dissolution of the Soviet Union, in September 1991, he was selected to head the centre, a position that he held until 2003. After his retirement, Klimuk served as an advisor to the president of Belarus. He was twice named Hero of the Soviet Union (1973, 1975).

VLADIMIR KOMAROV
(b. March 16, 1927, Moscow, Russia, U.S.S.R. [now Russia]—d. April 24, 1967, Kazakhstan)

Vladimir Mikhaylovich Komarov was the first man to have died during a space mission.

Komarov joined the Soviet Air Force at the age of 15 and was educated in air force schools, becoming a pilot in 1949. He graduated from the Zhukovsky Air Force Engineering Academy, Moscow, in 1959, and was the pilot (Oct. 12–13, 1964) of Voskhod 1, the first craft to carry more than one human being into space.

Komarov became the first Russian to make two spaceflights when he blasted off alone on April 23, 1967, in Soyuz 1. During the 18th orbit he attempted a landing. Reportedly, the spacecraft became entangled in its main parachute at an altitude of several miles and fell back to Earth. Komarov's body was cremated, and his ashes were entombed in the wall of the Kremlin.

SERGEY KRIKALYOV
(b. Aug. 27, 1958, Leningrad, Russia, U.S.S.R. [now Saint Petersburg, Russia])

The six spaceflights from 1988 to 2005 of Russian cosmonaut Sergey Konstantinovich Krikalyov have earned him the world record for most time in space.

After earning a degree in mechanical engineering from the Leningrad Technical Institute, Krikalyov joined NPO Energia (now RKK Energia), the largest Soviet spacecraft design organization, as an engineer in 1981 and became a civilian trainee cosmonaut four years later. He flew his first space mission in 1988–89 as flight engineer on Soyuz TM-7, during which he spent 151 days in space aboard the Mir space station. He was in the public eye in 1991–92 during his second mission, also to Mir, for being in space during the dissolution of the Soviet Union. Having been launched as a Soviet citizen, he returned 311 days later as a Russian citizen.

Krikalyov was the first Russian cosmonaut to serve aboard an American spacecraft. In 1994 he flew as a mission specialist aboard STS-60, a mission on the *Discovery* space shuttle lasting eight days.

Sergey Konstantinovich Krikalyov. NASA

He flew for a fourth time in space in 1998 as a mission specialist aboard STS-88, during which the *Endeavour* space shuttle visited the International Space Station (ISS). The flight lasted 12 days. His fifth space mission was in 2000–01, when he served as flight engineer on Soyuz TM-31 as part of the first resident crew (Expedition 1) on the ISS. He spent 141 days in space during this mission. In 2005 he went into space for the sixth time, to the ISS as commander on Soyuz TMA-6. As part of the crew of Expedition 11, he spent 179 days in space, thus accumulating 803 days total during his career. In

2007 he became vice president of manned flights at Energia but still remained an active cosmonaut.

VALERY KUBASOV
(b. Jan. 7, 1935, Vyazniki, U.S.S.R. [now Russia])

Valery Kubasov performed the first welding experiments in space. Upon graduating from the Moscow Aviation Institute in 1958, Kubasov worked for the design bureau of Soviet spacecraft designer Sergey Korolyov and was the author of studies on spaceship trajectories. In 1966 he was accepted into the cosmonaut program and began spaceflight training.

On Oct. 11, 1969, Kubasov made his first flight aboard Soyuz 6, where with the crews of Soyuz 7 and 8 he participated in the first group spaceflight. As flight engineer, Kubasov was the first person to weld in space. Kubasov was later chosen for the Soyuz 11 crew, which would man the first space station, Salyut 1. However, Kubasov was thought to have contracted tuberculosis, and his crew was grounded days before launch. On June 29, 1971, the cosmonauts who replaced Kubasov's crew died during reentry of Earth's atmosphere when their capsule accidentally decompressed.

In 1975 Kubasov returned to space on a mission that accomplished the first joint Soviet-American spaceflight. The Soyuz 19 linked with the American spaceship Apollo on July 17. Kubasov spent nearly five hours in the Apollo

Command and Docking modules. He launched on his final flight on May 26, 1980, as commander of Soyuz 36, an Intercosmos mission to the Salyut 6 space station with the first Hungarian cosmonaut, Farkas Bertalan. After his retirement from spaceflight, Kubasov became deputy director of the Russian spacecraft manufacturer RKK Energia.

ALEKSEY LEONOV
(b. May 30, 1934, near Kemerovo, Russia, U.S.S.R. [now Russia])

Aleksey Arkhipovich Leonov was the first man to climb out of a spacecraft in space.

After early schooling in Kaliningrad, Leonov joined the Soviet air force in 1953. He completed his flight training in 1957 and served as a fighter pilot until 1959, when he was selected for cosmonaut training.

On March 18, 1965, Voskhod 2 was launched into space with Leonov and Pavel Belyayev aboard. During the second orbit Leonov let himself out of the spacecraft by means of an air lock while about 110 miles (177 km) above the Crimea. Tethered to the ship, Leonov made observations, took motion pictures, and practiced maneuvering in free-fall for about 10 minutes before reentering Voskhod 2 over western Siberia. The ship landed after completing 17 orbits (26 hours) in space.

A decade later, Leonov was commander of the Soviet Soyuz craft that linked in orbit with the U.S. Apollo craft on July 17, 1975. Later in his career, he worked at the cosmonaut training centre.

ANDRIYAN NIKOLAYEV
(b. Sept. 5, 1929, Shorshely, Chuvash A.S.S.R., U.S.S.R. [now Chuvashia, Russia]—d. July 3, 2004, Cheboksary, Chuvashia, Russia)

Andriyan Grigoryevich Nikolayev piloted the Vostok 3 spacecraft, launched Aug. 11, 1962. When Vostok 4, piloted by Pavel R. Popovich, was launched a day later, there were, for the first time, two manned craft in space simultaneously. The two made radio and visual contact, but there was no attempt at docking. Both landed on August 15.

The son of a worker on a collective farm, Nikolayev studied and worked in forestry until drafted into the Soviet army in 1950. An early interest in flying persisted, and he soon transferred to the air force; in 1954 he became a pilot. In 1957 he joined the Communist Party, and in March 1960 he entered cosmonaut training. In 1962 he became the third Russian cosmonaut to travel into space, and during his 96-hour flight, which set an endurance record, he orbited Earth 64 times. Nikolayev later served as the commander of the Soviet Astronauts' Detachment.

On Nov. 3, 1963, Nikolayev married Valentina Tereshkova, who in June 1963 had become the first woman to travel in space. They had one child and were subsequently divorced.

Nikolayev and Vitaly I. Sevastyanov manned the Soyuz 9 flight on June 1, 1970, and set a new space endurance record of almost 18 days in orbit. The mission, primarily one of determining the effects of prolonged spaceflight, ended on June 19. Nikolayev was twice named Hero of the Soviet Union.

VIKTOR PATSAYEV

(b. June 19, 1933, Aktyubinsk, Kazakhstan, U.S.S.R. [now Aqtöbe, Kazakhstan]—d. June 29, 1971, in space)

Viktor Ivanovich Patsayev was design engineer on the Soyuz 11 mission, in which he, mission commander Georgy T. Dobrovolsky, and flight engineer Vladislav N. Volkov remained in space a record 24 days and created the first manned orbital scientific station by docking their Soyuz 11 spacecraft with the unmanned Salyut station launched two months earlier. The three were found dead in their space capsule after it made a perfect landing in Kazakhstan. The accident was caused by decompression resulting from a leak in their capsule when a hatch was improperly closed. While in the space station, they had conducted meteorological and plant-growing experiments.

VALERY POLYAKOV

(b. April 27, 1942, Tula, Russia, U.S.S.R. [now Russia])

Valery Vladimirovich Polyakov holds the record for the longest single spaceflight in history.

Valery Vladimirovich Polyakov. NASA

Polyakov had an early interest in spaceflight, and in 1971 he joined the Institute of Biomedical Problems in Moscow, the leading Soviet institution for space biomedicine. In 1972 he passed his exams to become one of the first doctor-cosmonaut trainees from the institute. He earned a Candidate of Medical Sciences degree in 1976.

After serving as reserve cosmonaut for several crews, Polyakov flew his first mission into space in 1988–89 as the doctor-cosmonaut on board Soyuz TM-6. During his 241-day flight aboard the Mir space station, he conducted numerous medical experiments.

After his mission, Polyakov returned to administrative duties before training for a second mission. He flew as doctor-cosmonaut of Soyuz TM-18 to the Mir space station in 1994. It was during this stay on Mir—from Jan. 8, 1994, to March 22, 1995—that he set the record of 438 days for the longest continuous stay in space.

In 1995 Polyakov formally retired as a cosmonaut, although he retained his duties as deputy director of the Institute for Biomedical Problems, a post to which he had been appointed in 1989. He simultaneously served as deputy chair of the commission in charge of certifying Russian cosmonauts.

PAVEL POPOVICH
(b. Oct. 5, 1930, Uzin, Ukraine, U.S.S.R. [now Ukraine])

Pavel Romanovich Popovich piloted the Vostok 4 spacecraft, launched Aug. 12, 1962. He and Andriyan G. Nikolayev, who was launched a day earlier in Vostok 3, became the first two men to be in space simultaneously.

Popovich, a herdsman in his early youth, graduated from a technical school in Magnitogorsk, Russia, U.S.S.R., in 1951, when he entered the army. He quickly transferred to the air force and in 1954 graduated from the Stalingrad Air Force College. He became a pilot, and in 1960 he was among the first to enter cosmonaut training.

Popovich was also the command pilot of the Soyuz 14 mission (July 3–19, 1974), on which he was accompanied by Yury P. Artyukhin. The cosmonauts docked their craft with Salyut 3, a space station that had been placed in orbit on June 25, and engaged in a 15-day program of scientific experiments.

SVETLANA SAVITSKAYA
(b. Aug. 8, 1948, Moscow, Russia, U.S.S.R. [now Russia])

Svetlana Yevgenyevna Savitskaya was the first woman to walk in space. The daughter of World War II fighter ace Yevgeny Savitsky, Savitskaya showed an aptitude for aviation at an early age. By her 22nd birthday, she had recorded over 400 parachute jumps and had claimed the top spot at the World Aerobatic Championships.

She earned an engineering degree from Moscow Aviation Institute in 1972 and was accepted as a test pilot candidate. She ultimately qualified to fly more than 20 different types of aircraft, earning a number of women's speed and altitude records in the process.

In 1980 Savitskaya was selected to join the Soviet space program, and she began training for work with Soyuz and Salyut spacecraft. On Aug. 19, 1982, as part of the Soyuz T-7 mission to the Salyut 7 space station, she became the second woman to enter outer space. On her second trip to Salyut 7, she became the first woman to perform a space walk when, on July 25, 1984, she participated in welding experiments on the outer hull of the space station.

Savitskaya returned to Earth and took an executive position at the aerospace design bureau Energia. She transitioned into politics, and in 1989 she was elected to the Duma as a member of the Communist Party. She remained active in the Duma throughout the reforms of the 1990s, and by 2003 she had risen to the fourth highest position in the Communist Party's ranks. She served as the deputy chairperson for the Duma's defense committee and won reelection to her seat in December 2007.

ANATOLY SOLOVYOV

(b. Jan. 16, 1948, Riga, Latvia, U.S.S.R. [now Latvia])

Anatoly Yakovlevich Solovyov flew into space five times and holds the record for the most time spent on space walks.

Solovyov, a fighter pilot who had served in the Soviet Far East, joined the Soviet cosmonaut squad as a trainee in 1976. He flew into space for the first time in 1988 as commander of the Soyuz TM-5 mission on a 10-day flight to the Mir space station with a Bulgarian "guest-cosmonaut," Aleksandr Aleksandrov.

In the early 1990s, Solovyov flew two long-duration missions to Mir, the first (Soyuz TM-9) lasting 179 days in 1990 and the second (Soyuz TM-15) lasting 189 days in 1992–93. During both flights, Solovyov, with his crewmates, conducted a total of six space walks to carry out repairs.

Solovyov played a key role in the cooperative shuttle-Mir missions in the early 1990s. In 1995 he and his crewmate were delivered to Mir aboard the space shuttle *Atlantis* (mission STS-71) for a 75-day stay on the station. He conducted three more space walks during this flight.

Although he was tapped to be on the first crew to the International Space Station, Solovyov declined to serve under an American commander. Instead, he flew his last space mission on Soyuz TM-26 in 1997–98, spending 198 days aboard Mir. With a grand total of 651 days in space, he became one of the most experienced space travelers of all time.

Anatoly Yakovlevich Solovyov. NASA

Solovyov retired from the cosmonaut squad in 1999. He became the president of For the Good of the Fatherland, a national organization that recognizes the work of Russians devoted to national social and cultural development.

GENNADY STREKALOV

(b. Oct. 28, 1940, Mytishchi, U.S.S.R. [now Russia]—d. Dec. 25, 2004, Moscow)

Gennady Mikhailovich Strekalov flew five times in space over a period of 15 years and participated in the first joint

Gennady Mikhailovich Strekalov playing guitar and singing with (from left to right) astronauts Charlie Precourt, Bonnie Dunbar, and Greg Harbaugh in June 1995 during the space shuttle's first visit to the Russian space station Mir. NASA

Russian-American flight to the Mir space station.

From 1957 Strekalov was a mechanic at the OKB-1 design organization (now known as RKK Energia) and worked on the first Sputnik satellite. In 1973 he formally joined the organization's engineer cosmonaut squad. He flew his first mission in 1980 as a cosmonaut-researcher on Soyuz T-3, a short repair flight to the Salyut 6 station lasting 13 days.

His two attempts to reach the Salyut 7 space station in 1983 ended in failure. In April the three-man Soyuz T-8 crew failed to dock with the station and returned to Earth after a two-day flight. In September the booster rocket for his Soyuz exploded on the pad prior to liftoff. Strekalov and his crewmate were saved by a rescue system. In 1984 he finally reached Salyut 7 as part of a visiting crew (on Soyuz T-11) that included an Indian guest-cosmonaut, Rakesh Sharma. The mission lasted eight days.

Strekalov flew two long-duration missions to the Mir space station, the first in 1990 and the second in 1995. During the first flight (Soyuz TM-10), lasting 131 days, he carried out one space walk. On his second trip (Soyuz TM-21), Strekalov flew with astronaut Norm Thagard, the first American to fly on a Russian space station. Strekalov and his crewmates spent 115 days in orbit, gaining valuable experience on joint flights between two vastly different technological cultures. He formally retired as a cosmonaut in 1995, although he remained a senior cosmonaut training official at RKK Energia.

VALENTINA TERESHKOVA
(b. March 6, 1937, Maslennikovo, Russia, U.S.S.R. [now Russia])

Valentina Vladimirovna Tereshkova was the first woman to travel into space. On June 16, 1963, she was launched in the spacecraft Vostok 6, which completed 48 orbits in 71 hours. In space at the same time was Valery F. Bykovsky, who had been launched two days earlier in Vostok 5; both landed on June 19.

Although she had no pilot training, Tereshkova was an accomplished amateur parachutist and on this basis was accepted for the cosmonaut program when she volunteered in 1961. She left the program just after her flight, and on Nov. 3, 1963, she was married to Andriyan G. Nikolayev, another cosmonaut.

From 1962 until 1990/91 she was an active member in the U.S.S.R. Supreme Soviet. She directed the Soviet Women's Committee in 1968, and from 1974 to 1990/91 she served as a member of the Supreme Soviet Presidium. Tereshkova was named a Hero of the Soviet Union and was twice awarded the Order of Lenin.

GHERMAN TITOV
(b. Sept. 11, 1935, Verkhneye Zhilino, near Barnaul, Russia, U.S.S.R. [now Russia]—d. Sept. 20, 2000, Moscow)

Gherman Stepanovich Titov piloted the Vostok 2 spacecraft, launched on Aug. 6, 1961, on the first manned spaceflight of more than a single orbit; Yury Gagarin had made the first orbit of Earth on April 12, 1961.

Titov was accepted in 1953 for aviation cadet training, graduating in 1957 as a jet fighter pilot from the Stalingrad Flying Academy. In 1960 he entered cosmonaut training, during the course of which he received the Order of Lenin for an engineering proposal and was selected as the backup cosmonaut to Gagarin for Vostok 1.

During the Vostok 2 flight of 25 hours 18 minutes, Titov was assigned the communications code name Eagle. His radio identification, "I am Eagle!," was spoken with intense excitement and made an impression on listeners around the world.

Following his flight Titov was named a Hero of the Soviet Union and received another Order of Lenin. In 1962 he became a deputy of the Supreme Soviet, a position that he held until 1970, and in 1968 he graduated from the Zhukovsky Air Force Engineering Academy. Titov became a major general in 1975. In subsequent years he worked as an assistant to the chief editor of the *Journal of Aviation and Cosmonautics.*

Following the fall of the Soviet Union in 1991, Titov entered politics and was elected to the Duma, the lower house of the Russian parliament, in 1995; he did not run for a second term in 1999. His writings in English translation include *I Am Eagle* (1962) and *Seventeen Cosmic Dawns* (1963).

ALEKSANDR VOLKOV
(b. April 27, 1948, Gorlovka, Donetsk oblast, Ukraine, U.S.S.R. [now Ukraine])

Aleksandr Aleksandrovich Volkov was the first cosmonaut whose son also went into space.

Volkov graduated from the Chuguyev Higher Air Force School in Kharkov province in Ukraine, U.S.S.R., in 1970. After graduation from the air force school, Volkov served as a test pilot in the Soviet air force and eventually reached the rank of colonel.

Volkov received cosmonaut training from 1976 to 1979. He first flew into space on Sept. 17, 1985, as a research cosmonaut aboard Soyuz T-14 to the Salyut 7 space station. While stationed on Salyut 7, Volkov and two fellow crew members, commander Vladimir Vasyutin and flight engineer Georgy Grechko, conducted scientific and technical experiments with military applications. Unfortunately, the mission was cut short due to the unexpected psychological illness of Vasyutin, and the crew returned to Earth aboard Soyuz T-14 on Nov. 21, 1985.

Volkov flew into space for a second time on Nov. 26, 1988, aboard the Soyuz TM-7 flight to the Mir space station. The crew of Soyuz TM-7 also included flight engineer Sergey Krikalyov of the Soviet Union and research cosmonaut Jean-Loup Chrétien of France. The cosmonauts conducted scientific experiments with the three cosmonauts who were already stationed on Mir, focusing their research efforts mostly on medical and technology experiments in support of the Hermes shuttle project of the European Space Agency. On Dec. 9, 1988, Volkov and Chrétien conducted a space walk to assemble an experimental deployable structure called ERA for French experiments. The mission was shortened due to delays in sending certain modules to Mir, which led to the decision to leave Mir uninhabited until the add-on modules were ready. Volkov returned to Earth aboard Soyuz TM-7 on April 27, 1989.

Volkov traveled into space for a third time on Oct. 2, 1991, as the commander of the Soyuz TM-13 flight to Mir with research cosmonauts Toktar Aubakirov of the Soviet Union and Franz Viehböck of Austria. The cosmonauts performed scientific and technical research, and Volkov conducted a space walk to dismantle equipment and recover experiment materials. He returned to Earth aboard Soyuz TM-13 on March 25, 1992, after nearly six months in space. Volkov's third space mission attracted considerable public attention due to the dissolution of the Soviet Union in December 1991, while Volkov was in space. He was launched into space as a Soviet citizen and returned to Earth 176 days later, landing in Kazakhstan in a Russian spacecraft.

Volkov was awarded the headtitle Hero of the Soviet Union and was bestowed with the Order of Lenin. He served as the commander of the cosmonaut detachment at the Yury Gagarin Cosmonaut Training Centre in Star City, Russia, from 1990 to 1998. He left the space service on Aug. 21,

1998, and retired from active duty in the Russian air force soon after. He is the father of Sergey Volkov, who became the first second-generation cosmonaut in history when he launched into space aboard Soyuz TMA-12 on April 8, 2008.

SERGEY VOLKOV
(b. April 1, 1973, Chuguyev, Kharkov oblast (region), Ukraine, U.S.S.R. [now Ukraine])

Military pilot Sergey Aleksandrovich Volkov was the first second-generation cosmonaut, following his father, Aleksandr Volkov, into space.

Volkov graduated from the Tambov Marina Raskova Air Force Academy for Pilots in Tambov, Russia, with a piloting and engineering degree in 1995. After completing his studies, Volkov entered the Russian air force and served as an assistant aircraft commander in military transport aviation.

In 1997 Volkov was selected as a cosmonaut candidate, and he received basic cosmonaut training until he qualified as a test cosmonaut in 1999. Beginning in January 2000 Volkov trained with the Russian Federal Space Agency as a Soyuz TMA commander and International Space Station (ISS) flight engineer, and he served as a member of the backup crew for several ISS missions. Volkov flew into space aboard Soyuz TMA-12 on April 8, 2008, with Russian flight engineer Oleg Kononenko and South Korean spaceflight participant Yi Soyeon as part of Expedition 17 to the ISS.

With that flight he became the first second-generation cosmonaut in history. His father had spent 391 days in space on three missions (in 1985, 1988, and 1991) and directed the Russian cosmonaut training program. Though sons had followed their fathers into the cosmonaut corps before, the Volkovs were the first father-and-son cosmonaut duo to fly into space.

Volkov spent 198 days in space, performing scientific and technical experiments and carrying out maintenance, service, and repair projects on the ISS and on Soyuz TMA-12. He also conducted two space walks, during which he and Kononenko inspected the Soyuz TMA-12 spacecraft, removed and installed scientific experiments, and installed a docking target for a Russian module scheduled for launch in 2009. As the ISS commander for Expedition 17, Volkov earned the distinction of being the youngest ISS commander to date. He returned to Earth aboard Soyuz TMA-12 on Oct. 24, 2008.

After his flight Volkov continued to serve in the Russian air force (with the rank of lieutenant colonel) and remained an active cosmonaut.

VLADISLAV VOLKOV

(b. Nov. 23, 1935, Moscow, Russia, U.S.S.R. [now Russia]—d. June 29, 1971, in space)

Vladislav Nikolayevich Volkov was a participant in the Soyuz 7 and 11 missions of 1969 and 1971, the second of which resulted in the death of three cosmonauts.

Son of an aviation design engineer, Volkov was educated at the Moscow Aviation Institute. On the Soyuz 7 mission, Volkov, acting as flight engineer, was accompanied by Anatoly V. Filipchenko; the two tested welding techniques in space and multiple launching. Volkov was again flight engineer on the Soyuz 11 mission commanded by Georgy T. Dobrovolsky and accompanied by Viktor I. Patsayev.

The three cosmonauts remained in space a record 24 days and created the first manned orbital scientific station by docking their Soyuz 11 spacecraft with the unmanned Salyut 1 station launched two months earlier. The three were found dead in their space capsule after it made a perfect landing in Kazakhstan; decompression, resulting from a leak in their capsule when a hatch was improperly closed, was given as the cause of death. While in the space station, the cosmonauts had performed meteorological and plant-growing experiments.

BORIS YEGOROV

(b. Nov. 26, 1937, Moscow, Russia, U.S.S.R. [now Russia]—d. Sept. 12, 1994, Moscow)

Physician Boris Borisovich Yegorov, with cosmonauts Vladimir M. Komarov and Konstantin P. Feoktistov, was a participant in the first multimanned spaceflight, that of Voskhod ("Sunrise") 1, on Oct. 12–13, 1964, and was also the first practicing physician in space.

Upon graduating in 1961 from the First Medical Institute, Moscow,

Yegorov joined the team of physicians who studied medical telemetry data from Soviet spaceflights. An expert on the sense-of-balance mechanism in the inner ear, he began training for the Voskhod 1 flight during the summer of 1964. During the flight (which, with an apogee of 254 miles [409 km], was then the highest attained by a manned capsule), Yegorov tested the effects of radiation, confinement, weightlessness, and various other conditions of spaceflight on himself and the other cosmonauts. The flight was the first undertaken in woolen clothes rather than the usual space suits. It was suggested at the time that a longer flight had been planned, which was why a doctor was included.

Yegorov was not a trained long-term professional cosmonaut and returned to medical practice. The medical information gained from the Voskhod 1 flight and subsequent research enabled Soviet scientists to make advances in adapting humans to long spaceflights.

CHAPTER 10

INTERNATIONAL ASTRONAUTS AND SPACEFLIGHT PARTICIPANTS

Manned spaceflight is no longer strictly the territory of the United States and Russia. Representatives from several nations have accepted the invitation to join astronauts and cosmonauts in space, as guests on U.S. and Russian spacecraft and the ISS. A handful of countries have built their own space programs.

AKIYAMA TOYOHIRO
(b. July 22, 1942, Tokyo, Japan)

Akiyama Toyohiro was a Japanese journalist and television reporter who was the first Japanese citizen and the first journalist to travel into space. Akiyama was also the first fare-paying civilian passenger (non-professional astronaut) to participate in a spaceflight.

Akiyama earned his bachelor's degree at the International Christian University in Mitaka, Tokyo. In 1966 he joined the Tokyo Broadcasting System (TBS), a Japanese television company, as a reporter. After working for the British Broadcasting Corporation World Service in London for four years (1967–71), he was transferred to the TBS Division of Foreign News and eventually served as the chief TBS correspondent in Washington, D.C., for four years (1984–88).

In August 1989 Akiyama was selected for cosmonaut training for a commercial flight to the Soviet Mir space station. His journey was sponsored by TBS. The exact terms of the deal were not revealed, but the Soviets claimed to have received $14 million (other estimates are in the range of $10–$12 million), and the total expense of the trip and the ensuing broadcast for TBS is thought to have exceeded $20 million. It was the first commercial space-flight in history.

Akiyama completed the cosmonaut training course at the Yury Gagarin Cosmonaut Training Centre in Star City, Russia, and flew into space aboard Soyuz TM-11 on Dec. 2, 1990. The mission, named Mir Kosmoreporter, lasted eight days, and Akiyama landed back on Earth on Soyuz TM-10 on Dec. 10, 1990. During the mission, Akiyama made daily television broadcasts for TBS, conducting live reports from the Mir space station.

After completing his spaceflight, Akiyama returned to TBS and eventu-ally served as the deputy director of the TBS News Division. He resigned from TBS in 1995.

IVAN BELLA
(b. May 25, 1964, Brezno, Czech. [now Slovakia])

Pilot and air force officer Ivan Bella was the first Slovak citizen to go into space. Bella graduated from the military high school in Banská Bystrica in 1983 and earned his university degree from the Czechoslovak air force academy in Košice in 1987. After completing his education, Bella joined the Czechoslovak air force as a pilot and served as a combat pilot at the 33rd Air Force Base in Malacky beginning

in 1993. He eventually attained the rank of lieutenant colonel in the Slovak air force and the rank of colonel in the Slovak army.

Bella entered space service in March 1998, when he was selected as a cosmonaut candidate for flights to the Mir orbital space station. He completed six months of cosmonaut training at the Yury Gagarin Cosmonaut Training Centre in Star City, Russia, between March and August 1998. He flew his only space mission as a research cosmonaut on Soyuz TM-29, which launched on Feb. 20, 1999, and docked with Mir on February 22. Bella was accompanied on Soyuz TM-29 by a Russian cosmonaut, Viktor Afanasiyev, and a French astronaut, Jean-Pierre Haigneré. The mission, named "Mir Štefánik" after the Slovak astronomer and general Milan Štefánik, lasted eight days.

Bella landed back on Earth aboard Soyuz TM-28 on February 28. During the mission, Bella conducted several medical experiments regarding radiation levels, metabolism, and hormones and also per-formed research to determine the survival prospects of Japanese quails during long-haul flights. Bella was among the last cosmonauts to visit Mir, which was put out of service in March 2001.

Beginning in 2004, Bella served as a military attaché for Slovakia in Moscow.

ROBERTA BONDAR
(b. Dec. 4, 1945, Sault Ste. Marie, Ont., Can.)

Roberta Lynn Bondar was the first Cana-dian woman and the first neurologist to travel into space. Bondar earned a B.Sc. in zoology and agriculture from the University of Guelph (1968), an M.Sc. in experimental pathology from the University of Western Ontario (1971), and a Ph.D. in neurobiology from the University of Toronto (1974) before receiving an M.D. from McMaster University, Hamilton, Ont., in 1977. She received further postgraduate medical training in neurology and neuroophthalmology before she was admitted as a fellow in neurology to the Royal College of Physicians and Surgeons of Canada in 1981.

In 1983 Bondar was chosen as one of the six original Canadian astronauts, and she began her astronaut training as a member of the Canadian Space Agency (CSA) in 1984. In early 1990 Bondar was selected to be a payload specialist for the first International Microgravity Laboratory Mission (IML-1), a manned Spacelab module aimed at investigating the effects of weightlessness on living organisms and materials processing. She flew into space as a payload specialist on the *Discovery* space shuttle during the STS-42 mission, launching into space on Jan. 22, 1992, and returning to Earth on January 30. During the eight-day mission, she and her six fellow astronauts conducted several life science and materials science experiments on Spacelab, focusing on the adaptability of the human nervous system to low gravity and analyzing the effects of microgravity on other living organisms, such as shrimp eggs, fruit fly eggs, and bacteria.

Bondar left the CSA in September 1992 to devote more time to her research interests. Her pioneering status as Canada's first woman astronaut and the first neurologist in space and her accomplishments in space medicine brought her numerous awards and led to her appointment as an Officer of the Order of Canada, Canada's highest civilian honour. In 2003 Bondar was appointed chancellor of Trent University in Peterborough, Ont. She is the author of four books containing her photography, including *Touching the Earth* (1994), about her spaceflight, and *The Arid Edge of Earth* (2006), about deserts.

JEAN-LOUP CHRÉTIEN
(b. Aug. 20, 1938, La Rochelle, France)

French astronaut Jean-Loup Chrétien was the first person from western Europe to go into space, aboard a Soviet flight to the Salyut 7 space station in June 1982. Chrétien flew a second Soviet mission to space station Mir in 1988 and then returned to Mir as a U.S.-trained astronaut aboard the space shuttle in 1997.

Chrétien graduated in 1961 from the French Air Force Academy at Salon-de-Provence in southeastern France. He ultimately became a brigadier general in the French air force. In 1962 he began his career as a fighter pilot and then a test pilot, and in 1980 he was assigned to the French space agency, Centre National d'Études Spatiales (CNES). After his 1982 Salyut flight he served as head of the

Jean-Loup Chrétien. Roberto Schmidt/AFP/Getty Images

CNES astronaut office, and he began training for a flight aboard the space shuttle in 1984– 85. His flight opportunity was postponed after the *Challenger* accident of 1986. After his first flight to Mir in 1988, Chrétien participated in training as a pilot of the Soviet space shuttle *Buran* in 1990– 93 before that program was canceled.

Chrétien returned to astronaut training with NASA in 1995. In addition to his 1997 flight to Mir, he worked closely with NASA on overall U.S.-Russian cooperative activities. An off-duty accident forced Chrétien to retire as an astronaut in 2001. He became senior vice president of research and development at Tietronix, a software engineering firm in Houston, Texas, and in 2002 he founded Tietronix Optics, an optical technology company in Lannion, France.

PEDRO DUQUE
(b. March 14, 1963, Madrid, Spain)

Spanish aeronautical engineer Pedro Duque was the first Spanish citizen to go into space. Duque received a degree in aeronautical engineering from the Universidad Politécnica de Madrid (UPM) in 1986. Following graduation, Duque joined Grupo Mecánica del Vuelo (GMV), a Spanish firm that provides services for the space industry, and later worked at the European Space Agency's (ESA's) European Space Operations Centre in Darmstadt, Ger., before being selected to join the ESA astronaut corps in May 1992. He trained at both the European Astronaut Centre in Cologne, Ger., and the Yury Gagarin Cosmonaut Training Centre in Star City, Russia, and he worked as the coordinator between the crew on board the Mir space station and European scientists during the Euromir 94 mission, a joint project between ESA and the Russian space agency.

In 1995 Duque was selected by NASA as an alternate payload specialist for the STS-78 mission and served as a crew interface coordinator on the ground during that mission in June and July 1996. After further training at the Johnson Space Center in Houston, he qualified for assignments in space as a mission specialist. He flew into space for the first time in 1998 as a mission specialist aboard the space shuttle *Discovery* on STS-95. The mission lasted nine days (October 29 to November 7) and was focused on the study of the Sun, as well as research on weightlessness. Duque was responsible for supervising and maintaining the ESA experimental modules and the scientific machinery on board.

In 2001 Duque was chosen to attend the first advanced training class for the International Space Station (ISS). In 2003 Duque flew for a second time in space, as flight engineer on Soyuz TMA-3 during the Cervantes mission to the ISS. During this 10-day mission (October 18 to 28), Duque visited the ISS during a crew changeover, launching with Expedition 8 and returning with Expedition 7.

After completing his second spaceflight, Duque worked at UPM as director of operations of the Spanish User Support and Operations Centre, and in 2008 he became chief executive officer of Deimos Imaging, a European satellite and geospatial imaging company based in Valladolid, Spain.

MUHAMMED FARIS
(b. May 26, 1951, Aleppo, Syria)

Pilot and air force officer Muhammed Ahmed Faris became the first Syrian citizen to go into space. After graduating from military pilot school at the Syrian air force academy near Aleppo in 1973, Faris joined the air force and eventually attained the rank of colonel. He also served as an aviation instructor and a specialist in navigation later in his military career. In 1985 he was chosen as one of two Syrian candidates to participate in the Intercosmos spaceflight program, which allowed cosmonauts from allied countries to participate in Soviet space missions. Faris reported to the cosmonaut training centre in Star City, Russia, for training on Sept. 30, 1985.

Faris flew into space as a research cosmonaut on board the Soyuz TM-3 spacecraft on July 22, 1987, as part of the first visiting crew to the Mir orbital space station. The three-man crew included, along with Faris, two Soviet cosmonauts, Aleksandr Viktorenko and Aleksandr P. Aleksandrov. During the mission, Faris conducted several research experiments with Soviet cosmonauts in the fields of space medicine and materials processing. He returned to Earth aboard Soyuz TM-2 on July 30, 1987, having spent a total of eight days in space.

After his mission, Faris returned to the Syrian air force and settled in Aleppo. For his accomplishments as a cosmonaut, he was awarded the headtitle Hero of the Soviet Union, and he also received the Order of Lenin, the Soviet Union's highest civilian decoration.

FARKAS BERTALAN
(b. Aug. 2, 1949, Gyulahza, Hung.)

Pilot Farkas Bertalan was the first Hungarian citizen to travel into space. Farkas graduated from the György Kilián Aeronautical College in Szolnok, Hung., in 1969 and then attended the Krasnodar Military Aviation Institute in Krasnodar, U.S.S.R. (now Russia), from which he

graduated in 1972. Farkas qualified as a first-class military pilot in the Hungarian air force in 1976.

Farkas was chosen as a cosmonaut candidate in 1978 as a member of the Intercosmos program's fifth international crew. The non-Soviet cosmonauts of Intercosmos flew alongside Soviet crews on missions intended to demonstrate unity between Warsaw Pact and other countries sympathetic to the Soviet Union. After completing his cosmonaut training at the Yury Gagarin Cosmonaut Training Centre in Star City, U.S.S.R. (now Russia), Farkas flew into space on May 26, 1980, as a research cosmonaut on Soyuz 36 with a Soviet cosmonaut, commander Valery Kubasov. Farkas took part in several medical, biological, physical, and materials science experiments on board the Salyut 6 space station. He returned from space aboard Soyuz 35, landing on Earth on June 3, 1980. He was awarded the headtitle Hero of the Soviet Union and received the Order of Lenin.

After his flight Farkas returned to the Hungarian air force. In subsequent years he worked as a scientist at the Technical University of Budapest (now known as the Budapest University of Technology and Economics) and received a degree from its faculty of transport engineering in 1986. Farkas later served as the air force attaché at the Hungarian embassy in Washington, D.C., from 1996 to 1997. He retired from the Hungarian air force as a brigadier general in 1997. After his retirement he served as president of Airlines

Service and Trade Ltd., in Budapest and co-owned Atlant-Hungary Airlines.

DIRK FRIMOUT
(b. March 21, 1941, Poperinge, Belg.)

Astrophysicist and astronaut Dirk Dries David Damiaan, Viscount Frimout, was the first Belgian citizen to travel into space. Frimout received a degree in electrotechnical engineering from the University of Ghent in 1963 and earned a doctorate there in applied physics in 1970. He did postgraduate work at the University of Colorado in Boulder for two years (1971–72) as a research fellow from the European Space Research Organization. Frimout worked at the Belgian Institute for Space Aeronomy for 13 years (1965–78), where he performed research with stratospheric balloons and sounding rockets.

Frimout was selected as an astronaut candidate by the European Space Agency in 1977. During his training he worked at the Microgravity Division of the European Space Research and Technology Centre in Noordwijk, Neth. He was nominated as an alternate payload specialist for the STS-61-K flight, but that mission was canceled after the *Challenger* disaster on Jan. 28, 1986. In October 1989 NASA selected him as the backup payload specialist for the STS-45 mission (a renamed version of STS-61-K). Frimout became a primary crew member on STS-45 when American payload specialist Michael Lampton experienced medical problems, and he flew his first space mission aboard the *Atlantis* space shuttle in 1992.

STS-45 launched on March 24, 1992. During the nine-day mission, the astronauts carried out 12 experiments with the Atmospheric Laboratory for Applications and Science (ATLAS-1) cargo and made extremely detailed measurements of the chemical and physical properties of the atmosphere. Frimout was in charge of supervising the European scientific experiments.

Frimout's status as the first Belgian to travel into space brought him immense fame. Upon his return to Belgium, he was made a Grand Officier de l'Ordre de Léopold and was ennobled with the head-title of viscount. Frimout later worked at Belgacom, a Belgian telecommunications company, as a director of research.

CHRISTER FUGLESANG
(b. March 18, 1957, Stockholm, Swed.)

Physicist and astronaut Arne Christer Fuglesang was the first Swedish citizen in space. Fuglesang earned a master's degree in engineering physics from the Royal Institute of Technology (KTH) in Stockholm in 1981 and received a doctorate in experimental particle physics from the University of Stockholm in 1987.

In May 1992 he was selected for the European Space Agency's (ESA's) astronaut corps and began training at the European Astronaut Centre in Cologne, Ger., and he later trained at the Yury Gagarin Cosmonaut Training Centre in Star City, Russia. After three months of specialized training on the operations of the Soyuz spacecraft, Fuglesang was selected by NASA for mission specialist training at the Johnson Space Center in Houston in August 1996.

Eight years after qualifying as a mission specialist, Fuglesang flew on his first space mission, STS-116, aboard the space shuttle *Discovery* on Dec. 9, 2006. The mission (named "Celsius" by ESA in honour of Anders Celsius, the 18th-century Swedish astronomer) took the astronauts to the International Space Station (ISS) for an assembly and crew-

Swedish citizen Christer Fuglesang put his engineering degree to work as he reworked the International Space Station's power system during a 2006 space walk. NASA/Getty Images

rotation assignment. During the 13-day mission, Fuglesang conducted two scheduled space walks in order to install new hardware for the ISS and to rewire its electrical power system. He later took part in a third, unscheduled, space walk to fix the faulty retraction system of a solar panel, spending more than 18 hours combined on space walks. *Discovery* returned to Earth on December 22.

In 2006 Fuglesang was appointed an affiliated professor at KTH, where he had taught mathematics since 1980.

MARC GARNEAU

(b. Feb. 23, 1949, Quebec city, Que., Can.)

Naval officer and astronaut Marc Garneau was the first Canadian citizen to go into space. Garneau received a B.S. in

Marc Garneau, 2000. NASA

engineering physics from the Royal Military College in Kingston, Ont., in 1970 and a doctorate in electrical engineering from Imperial College of Science and Technology in London, Eng., in 1973. He served as a Canadian naval officer from 1974 to 1989. In 1983 he was selected as one of the first six Canadian astronauts. He became the first Canadian in space when he flew aboard the U.S. space shuttle as a payload specialist in October 1984; on that flight, he operated several Canadian experiments. In 1989 Garneau retired from the military and became deputy director of the Canadian astronaut program.

In 1992 Garneau began astronaut mission specialist training with NASA in the United States. He made two more spaceflights in 1996 and 2000. On the 1996 STS-77 mission, Garneau once again was in charge of several Canadian experiments; on the STS-97 mission in 2000, which docked with the International Space Station (ISS), he operated the shuttle's robotic arm to help deploy the first set of solar arrays for the ISS. In February 2001 he became executive vice president of the Canadian Space Agency (CSA); in November of that year he became the agency's president. He resigned from the CSA in November 2005 in order to run for Parliament in a March 2006 election. He was defeated in this attempt, but he was later elected to Parliament in October 2008 as a member of the Liberal Party for the Montreal riding of Westmount–Ville-Marie.

JUGDERDEMIDIIN GURRAGCHA

(b. Dec. 5, 1947, Gurvan-Bulak, Mong.)

Jugderdemidiin Gurragcha was the first Mongolian and second Asian to go into space. Gurragcha studied aerospace engineering at the Zhukovsky Military Engineering Academy in Ulan Bator (now Ulaanbaatar), graduating in 1977. He joined the Mongolian air force as an aeronautical engineer and rose to the rank of major general.

In March 1978 he was selected to participate in the Soviet Union's eighth international Intercosmos mission. His first and only space mission was as a researcher on the Soyuz 39 mission. On March 22, 1981, he and Soviet cosmonaut Vladimir Dzhanibekov were launched into space from the Baikonur Cosmodrome in Kazakhstan. He spent nearly eight days in space, carrying out scientific experiments on the Soviet space station Salyut 6.

Gurragcha left the space program on March 30, 1981, and was awarded the headtitle Hero of the Soviet Union. He later became chief of staff of air defense for the Mongolian armed forces. From 2000 to 2004 he served as minister of defense.

CLAUDIE HAIGNERÉ

(b. May 13, 1957, Le Creusot, France)

Cosmonaut and doctor Claudie Haigneré (née André-Deshays) was the first French woman in space. Haigneré graduated as a rheumatologist from Faculté de Médecine and Faculté des Sciences in Paris and completed a doctorate in neurosciences in 1992. From 1984 to 1992 she worked at the Cochin Hospital in Paris in rheumatology and rehabilitation.

In 1985 she was selected as a candidate astronaut by the French space agency, Centre National d'Études Spatiales (CNES). After her selection she conducted research on the effect of space travel on human physiology, specifically the adaptation of cognitive and motor skills in a microgravity environment. In 1992 she was named the alternate to French cosmonaut Jean-Pierre Haigneré (whom she married in 2001) for "Altair," the Franco-Russian Soyuz TM-17 space mission, which launched in July 1993.

In 1994 Haigneré was selected for the Franco-Russian "Cassiope" mission and began training at the Yury Gagarin Cosmonaut Training Centre in Star City, Russia. On Aug. 17, 1996, she launched into space aboard Soyuz TM-24 with two Russian cosmonauts, commander Valery Korzun and flight engineer Aleksandr Kaleri, and docked with the Mir space station. She returned to Earth on Sept. 2, 1996, on Soyuz TM-23.

In 1999 she became the first woman qualified to command a Soyuz capsule during reentry. On Oct. 21, 2001, she became the first female European cosmonaut to take part in a flight to the International Space Station (ISS) when she served as flight engineer on Soyuz TM-33 with two Russian cosmonauts, commander Viktor Afanasiyev and flight engineer Konstantin Kozeyev. After nearly 10 days in space, her crew flew Soyuz TM-32 back to Earth on October 31, leaving the newer Soyuz TM-33 as an emergency craft for the ISS crew.

From 2002 to 2005 Haigneré served in several political positions in France, including minister for research and new technologies, minister for European affairs, and secretary-general for Franco-German cooperation. In November 2005 the European Space Agency chose her to be adviser to the director general.

MIROSŁAW HERMASZEWSKI
(b. Sept. 14, 1941, Lipniki, Wolynian Voivodshi, Pol.)

Pilot Mirosław Hermaszewski was the first Pole in space. A 1965 graduate of the military pilot school in Deblin, Hermaszewski entered the Polish air force and in 1971 graduated from the Karol Sverchevski Military Academy. In 1976 he was selected from a pool of 500 pilots to participate in the Soviet Union's Intercosmos program. The non-Soviet cosmonauts of Intercosmos flew alongside Soviet crews on missions intended to demonstrate unity among Warsaw Pact and other countries sympathetic to the Soviet Union. Hermaszewski's was the second Intercosmos mission, launched on June 27, 1978.

As a research cosmonaut on the Soyuz 30 mission, Hermaszewski spent nearly eight days in space, carrying out scientific experiments and photographing Earth's surface from the Salyut 6 space station. On July 5, 1978, the team returned to Earth, landing 300 km (200 miles) west of Tselinograd (now Astana, Kazakh.).

Hermaszewski became one of only a handful of non-Soviets to be named a Hero of the Soviet Union. He was awarded the Soviet Order of Lenin, the Polish Order of the Grunwald Cross (1st degree), and the Nicolaus Copernicus medal of the Polish Academy of Sciences. He returned to service in the Polish air force and in 1981 became a member of Poland's Military Council for National Salvation, a body that exercised governmental powers during the years of martial law. He graduated from the Voroshilov Military Academy in Moscow in 1982 before serving as the chief of the Shkola Orlyat High Aviation School and in the Defense Office of Poland.

In 1988 Hermaszewski was made a general and, before his retirement, was named second-in-command of the Headquarters of the Air Force.

GEORGY IVANOV
(b. Feb. 7, 1940, Lovech, Bulg.)

Cosmonaut Georgy Ivanov was the first Bulgarian in space. Ivanov (born Georgy Kakalov) graduated from the Bulgarian air force academy at Dolna in 1964 and served as an instructor at the academy before becoming a squadron commander of fighter aircraft in Bulgaria's air force in 1967.

In 1978 he was selected to participate in the Soviet Union's Intercosmos program. An unusual circumstance of his selection was that the Soviet government required him to change his surname from Kakalov to Ivanov, owing to the obscene connotations of the word "Kakalov" in Russian.

In the Intercosmos program, non-Soviet cosmonauts flew alongside experienced Soviet crews on routine missions in order to demonstrate solidarity with states sympathetic to the Soviet Union. Ivanov's Soyuz 33 mission, however, diverged sharply from routine. Soyuz 33 was launched as planned on April 10, 1979, but while approaching space station Salyut 6, the craft suffered engine failure. The crew's only chance of survival depended on manually igniting a reserve engine that possibly had been damaged during the malfunction. After a day spent in orbit, commander Nikolay Rukavishnikov succeeded in igniting the engine, and the Soyuz touched down 180 km (112 miles) outside its landing area.

Despite the failure of the mission, Ivanov was named a Hero of the Soviet Union and awarded the Order of Lenin, the Soviet Union's highest civilian honour. He returned to military service in Bulgaria, earned a doctorate in aerospace engineering, and was elected to the National Assembly, where he participated in the creation of Bulgaria's first democratic constitution in 1991. He also became managing director of Air Sofia, a Bulgarian air cargo company.

SIGMUND JÄHN
(b. Feb. 13, 1937, Morgenröthe-Rautenkranz, Vogtland, Ger.)

East German cosmonaut Sigmund Jähn was the first German in space. As a young man Jähn trained to become a printer, but in 1955 he joined the East German air force, where he became a pilot and a military scientist. In 1966 he left East Germany to study at the Gagarin Military Air Academy in the Soviet Union. Upon completing his studies, he worked in pilot education and flight safety and applied his fluency in Russian to translating a number of Soviet military and political publications into German.

In 1976 Jähn was selected to train as the first cosmonaut in the Soviet Intercosmos program. This program placed non-Soviet cosmonauts on routine flights with experienced Soviet cosmonauts in a campaign to demonstrate Soviet solidarity with Warsaw Pact states and other sympathetic countries. On Aug. 26, 1978, Jähn lifted off with Soviet cosmonaut Valery Bykovsky aboard Soyuz 31. On the space station Salyut, he conducted scientific experiments before returning to Earth on Soyuz 29 on Sept. 3, 1978.

Following the Intercosmos mission, Jähn was named a Hero of the Soviet Union and awarded the Order of Lenin, the Soviet Union's highest civilian honour. His home country of East Germany elevated him to a kind of socialist folk hero and proclaimed proudly that the first German in space had been not a West German but an East German citizen. In 1983 Jähn earned a Ph.D. in geophysics from the Central Institute for Physics of the Earth, at Potsdam. After the reunification of Germany, he represented the country and the European Space Agency as a consultant at the Yury Gagarin Cosmonaut Training Centre in Star City, Russia.

LEONID KADENYUK

(b. Jan. 28, 1951, Klishkovtsy, U.S.S.R. [now Ukraine])

Cosmonaut Leonid Kadenyuk flew on the U.S. space shuttle *Columbia* and was the first Ukrainian citizen in space. Upon graduating from the Chernihiv Higher Air Force School in 1971, Kadenyuk became a flight instructor until his enrollment in 1976 at the Air Force Cosmonaut Training Centre. Although he graduated from the Yury Gagarin Cosmonaut Training Centre in Star City in 1978, nearly 20 years passed before Kadenyuk's first spaceflight, which ironically was not aboard the Soviet Soyuz craft for which he trained as a flight engineer but aboard an American space shuttle.

While in the cosmonaut program, Kadenyuk received flight training in numerous types of craft, including the Soyuz, the Soyuz-TM, the Salyut space station, and the Mir orbital complex. He trained as commander for the *Buran* orbiter and is credited with having improved that craft's landing and lowering trajectories. As a test pilot he mastered 54 types of aircraft, and in 1989 he earned a master's degree in mechanical engineering from the Moscow Aviation Institute. Kadenyuk's

training also included studies in biology and botany, with an emphasis on scientific experimentation in microgravity.

In 1996 he joined the Institute of Botany at the National Academy of Sciences of Ukraine as part of a Ukrainian-American space biology collaboration. On Nov. 19, 1997, Kadenyuk flew as a payload specialist aboard the space shuttle *Columbia* on the STS-87 mission, where he conducted experiments to observe the effect of weightlessness on plant growth and biomass. Kadenyuk was later appointed adviser to the Ukrainian president on aviation and aeronautics and in 2002 was elected to the Ukrainian parliament, where he served as vice-chairperson of the National Security and Defense Committee.

FRANCO MALERBA

(b. Oct. 10, 1946, Genoa, Italy)

Biophysicist Franco Egidio Malerba was the first Italian to travel into space. Malerba received a B.S. in engineering (with a specialization in telecommunications) from the University of Genoa in 1970. After doing research at the Italian National Research Council's Cybernetics and Biophysics Laboratory in Genoa and at the U.S. National Institutes of Health in Bethesda, Md., he earned a doctorate in physics (with a specialization in biophysics) from the University of Genoa in 1974. He served in the Italian navy between 1974 and 1975.

In 1977, the European Space Agency (ESA) selected Malerba as one of four payload specialist candidates for the first

Spacelab mission on board the U.S. space shuttle. He worked as a research scientist in the space plasma physics division of ESA's European Space Research and Technology Centre in Noordwijk, Neth., for the next three years (1977–80). Malerba was also employed by the American company Digital Equipment Corporation in technical and management positions for 13 years (1976–89).

Malerba was chosen for payload specialist training by the Italian Space Agency (ASI) and by NASA in 1989. He flew into space on July 31, 1992, on the space shuttle *Atlantis* as the prime payload specialist on the STS-46 mission. Unfortunately, the mission's primary payload, the joint NASA/ASI Tethered Satellite System, was deployed only to 256 metres (840 feet) of its full extent of 20 km (13 miles) owing to technical problems with a jammed tether line. STS-46 returned to Earth on Aug. 8, 1992.

Between 1994 and 1999 Malerba served as a member of the European Parliament (MEP) in the European People's Party, a Christian-Democratic group. Malerba was also involved in the local government of Genoa from 1997 to 1999.

ARNALDO TAMAYO MÉNDEZ
(b. Jan. 29, 1942, Guantánamo, Cuba)

Cosmonaut Arnaldo Tamayo Méndez was the first Latin American, the first person of African descent, and the first Cuban to fly in space. After the revolution of 1959, Tamayo Méndez joined the Cuban air force as a pilot. In 1961 he went to the Soviet Union for training on the MiG-15, and during the Cuban missile crisis of 1962, he flew 20 reconnaissance missions.

Tamayo Méndez was selected as a cosmonaut candidate in March 1978 as part of the Soviet Union's Intercosmos program, which allowed guest cosmonauts from Warsaw Pact and other countries to participate in Soviet space missions. After completing cosmonaut training, Tamayo Méndez traveled into space aboard Soyuz 38 with Soviet cosmonaut Yury Romanenko on Sept. 18, 1980.

During the eight-day mission, Soyuz 38 docked with the Salyut 6 space station, and Tamayo Méndez and Romanenko conducted several scientific experiments and research studies. Upon his return Tamayo Méndez was awarded the first headtitle of Hero of the Republic of Cuba by Fidel Castro and was also bestowed with the Order of Lenin and the headtitle of Hero of the Soviet Union, the highest decoration in the Soviet Union.

After his spaceflight Tamayo Méndez returned to the Cuban air force. In 1982 he was appointed chairman of the Military-Patriotic Educational Society (SEPMI), a military instruction program for Cuban youth. He remained SEPMI's chairman until 1992. Tamayo Méndez eventually rose to the rank of brigadier general in the air force and served as the director of the Department of International Affairs for the Cuban armed forces and as the director of Cuba's civil defense organization. In 1980 he became a member of the Cuban legislature, the National Assembly of People's Power.

ULF MERBOLD

(b. June 20, 1941, Greiz, Ger.)

German physicist Ulf Merbold was the first European Space Agency (ESA) astronaut to go into space, as a payload specialist aboard the U.S. Spacelab-1 flight from Nov. 28 to Dec. 8, 1983. He was also the first ESA astronaut to fly to the Russian space station Mir, in 1994.

Merbold received a doctorate in science in 1976 from Stuttgart University and worked at the Max Planck Institute for Metals Research in Stuttgart. He specialized in both solid-state and low-temperature physics. In 1977 he was selected by ESA from among 1,800 applicants as one of

Ulf Merbold. NASA

three candidates for flight aboard the Spacelab-1 mission. His 1983 flight made him the first non-American to fly aboard the space shuttle. During this 11-day mission, he and his colleagues carried out 72 experiments in eight scientific disciplines.

Merbold was selected in 1988 as an ESA payload specialist for the International Microgravity Laboratory-1 Spacelab mission, which flew in January 1992. He then entered training for the first cooperative ESA-Russian mission on space station Mir. The 32-day Euromir 94 mission took place from Oct. 3 to Nov. 4, 1994.

Following his 1994 flight, Merbold continued to work with ESA. He left the European astronaut corps in 1999 and until 2004 was responsible for promoting the utilization of the International Space Station for microgravity research. He retired from ESA in 2005.

ABDUL AHAD MOHMAND

(b. Jan. 1, 1959, Sardah, Afg.)

Pilot Abdul Ahad Mohmand was the first Afghan citizen to travel into space. Mohmand was educated in Afghanistan and later attended the Gagarin Military Air Academy in Monino, U.S.S.R. (now Russia), in 1987. After graduation, Mohmand served in the Afghan air force, eventually reaching the rank of colonel.

In February 1988, Mohmand became a cosmonaut candidate for a flight to the Mir space station. Mohmand was originally the backup to another Afghan cosmonaut, Mohammad Dauran Ghulam

Masum, on the Soyuz TM-6 mission, but he replaced Masum on the primary flight crew when the latter was disqualified owing to appendicitis.

After completing his cosmonaut training, Mohmand launched into space as a research cosmonaut on Aug. 29, 1988, with two Soviet cosmonauts, commander Vladimir Lyakhov and research doctor Valery Polyakov. At the Mir space station, Mohmand conducted joint research experiments with Lyakhov and Polyakov and made observations of Afghanistan from space.

Mohmand and Lyakhov left Mir on September 6 aboard Soyuz TM-5. The initial landing attempt failed owing to sunlight interference that caused confusion in the infrared horizon sensors. Lyakhov ordered the computer to make another retrofire attempt, which was unsuccessful. Mohmand had been trained not to disturb Lyakhov when flying the Soyuz. However, Mohmand noticed that the Soyuz computer was proceeding with the first landing attempt and was one minute away from jettisoning the rocket engine that they would need to return to Earth. Mohmand pointed this out to Lyakhov, who stopped the descent program.

The crew spent another 24 hours under difficult and dangerous conditions in the descent module before succeeding in their last-chance deorbit and returning safely to Earth on September 7. Mohmand spent nearly nine days in space and was awarded the Order of Lenin and the head-title Hero of the Soviet Union.

Because it occurred at the height of the Soviet occupation of Afghanistan, Mohmand's flight to Mir and his status as the first Afghan citizen in space (aboard a Soviet spacecraft) carried significant symbolic importance. After the withdrawal of Soviet forces from Afghanistan, Mohmand became a political refugee. He eventually settled in Stuttgart, Ger., and became a German citizen.

MOHRI MAMORU
(b. Jan. 29, 1948, Yoichi, Hokkaido, Japan)

Mohri Mamoru was the first Japanese astronaut to go into space. He flew as a payload specialist aboard the Spacelab-J mission of the U.S. space shuttle in September 1992.

Mohri received bachelor and master of science degrees in chemistry from Hokkaido University in Sapporo and in 1976 received a doctorate in chemistry from Flinders University of South Australia in Adelaide. He served for 10 years on the faculty of Hokkaido University, beginning in 1975, with special interest in the fields of surface physics and chemistry.

He was selected in 1985 by the National Space Development Agency (NASDA) of Japan as one of the first three Japanese astronauts. While awaiting a flight assignment, he worked at the Center for Microgravity and Material Research at the University of Alabama, Huntsville, for two years. After his eight-day flight in 1992, on which he assisted

Mohri Mamoru, right before the takeoff of space shuttle mission STS-99, Feb. 11, 2000. NASA

in the conduct of 44 experiments in life sciences and materials processing, Mohri became head of the NASDA astronaut office. Mohri entered full astronaut training at NASA's Johnson Space Center in Houston in 1996. He flew as a mission specialist aboard the Shuttle Radar Topography Mission in February 2000.

In July 2001 Mohri became the first director of the Museum of Emerging Science and Innovation in Tokyo.

MUKAI CHIAKI
(b. May 6, 1952, Tatebayashi, Gumma ken (prefecture), Japan)

Doctor Mukai Chiaki was the first Japanese woman to travel into space. Mukai earned a doctorate in medicine in 1977 and a doctorate in physiology in 1988 from Keiō University School of Medicine in Tokyo.

Mukai was working as a heart surgeon in Japan when the National Space Development Agency of Japan (NASDA) in 1985 chose her as one of three payload specialist candidates for the STS-47/Spacelab-J mission, but she did not fly on that mission. She flew into space for the first time as a payload specialist on the STS-65 mission aboard the space shuttle *Columbia* on July 8, 1994. Mukai took part in several scientific and medical experiments, which were housed in a Spacelab module in *Columbia*'s cargo bay. STS-65 returned to Earth on July 23, 1994, after having spent 15 days in space.

After serving as a backup payload specialist on the STS-90 mission in 1998, Mukai traveled into space for a second time aboard the *Discovery* space shuttle on Oct. 29, 1998, as a payload specialist on the STS-95 mission. On this mission, the crew conducted more than 80 scientific experiments related to medical and materials research in a microgravity environment. (In particular, Mercury astronaut John Glenn flew as the other payload specialist and thereby allowed an examination of spaceflight and aging.)

Mukai became the first Japanese citizen to fly twice in space; STS-95 landed safely on Nov. 7, 1998.

During her service as a NASDA astronaut at NASA, Mukai also worked at the Baylor College of Medicine in Houston and at the Keiō University School of Medicine. In 2000 Mukai was the deputy mission scientist for the STS-107 mission, which flew in January 2003 and ended in tragedy when the space shuttle *Columbia* disintegrated and the crew perished during atmospheric reentry.

RODOLFO NERI VELA
(b. Feb. 19, 1952, Chilpancingo, Guerrero estado (state), Mex.)

Scientist and engineer Rodolfo Neri Vela was the first Mexican citizen to fly into space. Neri Vela earned a B.S. in mechanical and electronic engineering, specializing in communications technology, from the National Autonomous University of Mexico (UNAM) in 1975. After receiving an M.S. degree, with a specialization in telecommunications systems, from the University of Essex in Colchester, Eng., in 1976, he earned a doctorate in electromagnetic radiation from the University of Birmingham in England in 1979.

Neri Vela returned to Mexico and worked for the Radiocommunications Group at the Institute of Electrical Research in Cuernavaca, Morelos estado (state), Mex. He also served as the head of the Department of Planning and Engineering of the Morelos Satellite Program at the Mexican Ministry of Communications and Transportation and as a full-time postgraduate lecturer and researcher at UNAM.

Neri Vela was a payload specialist on the space shuttle *Atlantis* as part of the STS-61-B crew, which launched on Nov. 26, 1985. He spent seven days in space. During the mission, Neri Vela and his fellow crew members deployed three communications satellites, one of which was the Mexican satellite Morelos-B. Neri Vela also performed multiple scientific experiments for the Mexican government.

Neri Vela was later employed by the European Space Agency in The Netherlands (1989–90), where he worked on planning a section of the International Space Station. He has also published a number of books on space.

CLAUDE NICOLLIER
(b. Sept. 2, 1944, Vevey, Switz.)

Test pilot and astronaut Claude Nicollier was the first Swiss citizen to travel into space. Nicollier qualified as a pilot in the Swiss air force in 1966. He earned a B.S. in physics from the University of Lausanne in 1970. He attended the Swiss Air Transport School in Zürich and qualified as an airline pilot in 1974, receiving an assignment as a DC-9 pilot for Swissair. He earned a M.Sc. degree in astrophysics from the University of Geneva in 1975.

Nicollier joined the European Space Agency's (ESA's) space science department in 1976, working as a research scientist at its facilities in Noordwijk, Neth. In 1978 ESA selected him as a candidate for a payload specialist seat on the first Spacelab mission. In July 1980 Nicollier was dispatched to NASA's Johnson Space Center in Houston, where he received mission specialist training with other NASA astronaut candidates.

Nicollier served as a mission specialist on four flights, logging a total of more than 42 days in space. On STS-46 he flew on the space shuttle *Atlantis*, which launched into space on July 31, 1992, and returned on August 8. During the eight-day mission, the crew deployed the European Retrievable Carrier science platform and conducted the first test flight of the Tethered Satellite System, which deployed only to 256 metres (840 feet) of its full extent of 20 km (12 miles) owing to technical problems with a jammed tether line.

STS-61 on the space shuttle *Endeavour*, which lasted from Dec. 2 to Dec. 13, 1993, was the first servicing and repair mission to the Hubble Space Telescope (HST). Nicollier and the crew fixed an optical defect that was causing fuzzy images and restored the telescope to its full capacity. His third flight was on the STS-75 mission, which lasted 15 days on the *Columbia* space shuttle, launching on Feb. 22, 1996, and returning on March 9. The astronauts conducted numerous microgravity experiments during the mission, including an investigation of the formation of dendrites in metal and an examination of how metals solidify in microgravity.

Nicollier's final spaceflight took place between Dec. 19 and 27, 1999, on the STS-103 mission aboard the *Discovery* space shuttle; this was another repair and servicing mission to the HST. Nicollier participated in his first space walk during this mission, installing a new computer and one of three fine-guidance sensors to the HST. He become the first European to spacewalk on a shuttle flight.

Although he was technically based at ESA's European Astronaut Centre in Cologne, Ger., Nicollier remained at NASA's Astronaut Office until the end of his astronaut career, performing numerous technical assignments there. He served as the head of the Astronaut Office's Robotics branch from 1996 to 1998. In 2000 Nicollier was assigned to the Extravehicular Activity (EVA) branch, which was in charge of space walks, and he also served as the lead ESA astronaut in Houston.

Nicollier retired from the Swiss air force as a captain in 2004 and from ESA in 2007. In 2004 he started teaching at the École Polytechnique Fédérale in Lausanne, Switz., where he became a full professor in the electrical engineering department in 2007. He also held a concurrent appointment as a full professor in the school's Space Center.

WUBBO OCKELS
(b. March 28, 1946, Almelo, Neth.)

Physicist and astronaut Wubbo Johannes Ockels was the first Dutch citizen to travel into space. Ockels studied physics and mathematics at the University of Groningen, earning a doctorate in 1978. His thesis was based on his work at the Nuclear Physics Accelerator Institute, a research centre at the University of Groningen where he worked from 1973 to 1978.

The European Space Agency (ESA) selected Ockels in 1978 as one of three candidates for space shuttle missions involving Spacelab, ESA's manned research module. He was assigned to the Spacelab-1 mission. He began basic astronaut training at NASA's Johnson Space Center in Houston in May 1980 and completed his training in August 1981.

Ockels served as a ground communicator and liaison-scientist for the crew on board the space shuttle *Columbia* during the STS-9/Spacelab-1 mission in 1983. He flew into space aboard the *Challenger* space shuttle on Oct. 30, 1985, as a payload specialist on STS-61A, a German D-1 Spacelab mission. With eight crew members, the mission was the largest to fly into space. The mission also was notable for being the first in which some mission operations were controlled from outside the United States, with the German Space Operations Centre in Oberpfaffenhofen conducting the scientific operations. The crew completed more than 75 scientific experiments, conducting basic and applied microgravity research in diverse fields such as materials science, physiological sciences, biology, communications, and navigation. *Challenger* returned to Earth on Nov. 6, 1985.

In 1986 Ockels was assigned to the European Space Research and Technology Centre in Noordwijk, Neth., where he worked on human spaceflight projects until 1996. During this time Ockels was involved with the Columbus program, a European project to build a research module for the International Space Station. In 1992 he began teaching at the Delft University of Technology in Delft, Neth., and in 2003 he was made a full professor of aerospace for sustainable engineering and technology.

MARCOS PONTES
(b. March 11, 1963, Bauru, Braz.)

Pilot and astronaut Marcos Cesar Pontes was the first Brazilian citizen in space. Pontes graduated in 1984 as a military pilot with a B.S. in aeronautical technology from the Brazil Air Force Academy in Pirassununga. For 14 years he investigated aeronautical accidents as a flight safety officer. He earned a B.S. in aeronautical engineering from the Aeronautical Institute of Technology, in São Jose dos Campos, in 1993 and then completed a test-pilot course. He worked in the fields of missile testing, weapons development, and aircraft evaluation as a test pilot. Pontes graduated with distinction from the U.S. Naval Postgraduate School in Monterey, Calif., in 1998 with an M.S. in systems engineering.

In 1998 he was selected as a mission specialist and reported to NASA's Johnson Space Center in Houston, where he attended astronaut training. However, after space shuttle flights were put on hold by the 2003 *Columbia* disaster, Brazil reached an agreement in 2005 with Russia to send Pontes to space aboard a Russian craft. He launched from Kazakhstan on March 30, 2006, aboard Soyuz TMA-8 with commander Pavel Vinogradov of Russia and flight engineer Jeffrey Williams of the United States. During the eight-day mission to the International Space Station (ISS), he conducted several scientific experiments, including a study on the human body's reaction to spending prolonged periods in space. He returned to Earth on April 8, 2006, on Soyuz TMA-7. After his flight Pontes worked at the Johnson Space Center, where he was involved in the production of Brazilian parts for the ISS.

DUMITRU PRUNARIU

(b. Sept. 27, 1952, Brasov, Rom.)

Pilot and cosmonaut Dumitru Dorin Prunariu was the first Romanian citizen in space. Prunariu earned a degree in aerospace engineering from the Polytechnic University in Bucharest in 1976. In 1978 he became a senior lieutenant in the air force and was selected for spaceflight training as part of the Intercosmos program. The non-Soviet cosmonauts of Intercosmos flew alongside Soviet crews on missions intended to demonstrate unity between Warsaw Pact and other countries sympathetic to the Soviet Union.

Prunariu finished his training at the top of his class and was chosen to accompany Soviet cosmonaut Leonid Popov for a joint spaceflight. Prunariu and Popov launched on May 14, 1981, aboard Soyuz 40 and docked with the space station Salyut 6. The crew spent nearly eight days in space conducting experiments in the fields of biology, medicine, and physics. They returned to Earth on May 22, 1981.

Prunariu returned to the Romanian air force as the chief inspector for aerospace activities and taught courses in aerospace engineering at the Polytechnic University. From 1992 to 1995 he was the secretary of the Romanian Space Agency (ASR). He was also the chief inspector for aerospace activities on the General Staff of Aviation and Air Defense from 1991 to 1998. In 1999 he graduated from the National Defense College in Bucharest with a Ph.D. in spaceflight dynamics. From 1998 to 2004 he was president of the ASR, and from 2004 to 2005 he was the Romanian ambassador to Russia and chair of the Scientific and Technical Subcommittee of the United Nations Committee on Peaceful Exploration of Outer Space.

ILAN RAMON

(b. June 20, 1954, Ramat Gan, Israel—d. Feb. 1, 2003, over Texas, U.S.)

Israeli pilot Ilan Ramon was Israel's first astronaut and a payload specialist on the space shuttle *Columbia*'s final flight. Ramon, a graduate of the Israel Air Force Flight School, was a fighter pilot in the

1973 Yom Kippur War and in the 1982 military operations in Lebanon; he also took part in the 1981 bombing of an Iraqi nuclear reactor. He was selected for the U.S. astronaut program in 1998.

VLADIMÍR REMEK
(b. Sept. 26, 1948, České Budějovice, Czech. [now in Czech Republic])

Pilot and cosmonaut Vladimír Remek was the first person in space who was not from the Soviet Union or the United States and the first Czech citizen in space.

After graduating from aviation school as a lieutenant in 1970, Remek began active service for the Czechoslovak air force. From 1972 to 1976 he continued his studies at the Gagarin Air Force Academy in Monino, U.S.S.R. (now Russia). In 1976 he joined the Soviet cosmonaut unit as part of the Intercosmos program.

On March 2, 1978, he took off aboard Soyuz 28 as a research cosmonaut along with Soviet cosmonaut Aleksey Gubarev. The crew docked with the Salyut 6 space station, where the cosmonauts conducted scientific research and experiments. After nearly eight days in space, Remek and Gubarev returned to Earth on March 10.

He returned to the Czechoslovak air force, where he served as assistant to the chief of the Military Research Institute for six years. In 1985 he joined the Defense Office of Czechoslovakia, and he stayed there until 1989, when he left to work for an air and space museum in Prague. In

2004 Remek was elected to the European Parliament as a member of the Czech Communist Party delegation.

SALMĀN ĀL SAʿŪD
(b. June 27, 1956, Riyadh, Saudi Arabia)

Prince Sulṭān ibn Salmān ibn ʿAbd al-ʿAzīz Āl Saʿūd was the first Saudi Arabian citizen, the first Arab, the first Muslim, and the first member of a royal family to travel into space.

Educated in the United States, Salmān received a degree in mass communications from the University of Denver and earned a master's degree in social and political science from the Maxwell School of Citizenship and Public Affairs at Syracuse University. He later worked at the Ministry of Information in Saudi Arabia as a researcher and served as the deputy director for the Saudi Arabian Olympic Information Committee at the 1984 Olympics in Los Angeles. In 1985 he was commissioned as an officer in the Royal Saudi Air Force and served as a fighter pilot. He retired from military service with the rank of colonel.

Later that year Salmān was chosen by NASA as a payload specialist for the STS-51G space shuttle mission. He embarked on an abbreviated training schedule, and on June 17, 1985, Salmān flew on the space shuttle *Discovery* as part of a seven-member international crew. During the seven-day mission, Salmān represented the Arab Satellite Communications Organization (ARABSAT) and took part in the deployment of the organization's satellite, ARABSAT-1B.

While in space, he also carried out a series of experiments that had been designed by Saudi scientists, including an ionized gas experiment set up by another member of the Saudi royal family for his Ph.D. dissertation and an experiment concerning the behaviour of oil and water when mixed in zero gravity. Salmān also spoke to his uncle, King Fahd, by telephone while in space and conducted a guided tour of the space shuttle's interior in Arabic, which was broadcast on television channels in the Middle East. The shuttle landed back on Earth on June 24, 1985.

Upon his return, Salmān became a founding member of the Association of Space Explorers, an international organization for astronauts and cosmonauts who have traveled into space, and served on its board of directors. His unique accomplishments brought him numerous state honours, particularly from Muslim and Arab countries such as Pakistan, Kuwait, Qatar, Bahrain, Morocco, and Syria.

Salmān was appointed as the first secretary-general of the Supreme Tourism Commission in Saudi Arabia when the organization was formed in 2000. In this position, he worked to expand and enhance the tourism sector in his country by playing a leading role in developing the country's tourism strategy and devising the industry's regulations. In 2008 his term of service was extended at a ministerial rank for another four years.

RAKESH SHARMA
(b. Jan. 13, 1949, Patiala, Punjab state, India)

Rakesh Sharma was the first Indian citizen in space. In 1970 Sharma joined the Indian air force as a pilot. He flew 21 combat missions in a MiG-21 in the Bangladesh war of 1971. In 1982 he was selected as a cosmonaut for a joint Soviet-Indian spaceflight.

On April 3, 1984, he flew on board Soyuz T-11 with two Soviet cosmonauts, commander Yury Malyshev and flight engineer Gennady Strekalov, to the space station Salyut 7. There Sharma performed experiments that included photography of India from space and exercises to study the effects of yoga on the body during weightlessness. The mission lasted nearly eight days, and Sharma and his crewmates landed in Kazakhstan on April 11.

In 1987 he joined the Indian company Hindustan Aeronautics as its chief test pilot. He left Hindustan Aeronautics in 2001 and became chairman of the board of Automated Workflow, a process-management company based in Bangalore (Bengaluru).

HELEN SHARMAN
(b. May 30, 1963, Sheffield, Eng.)

Chemist Helen Patricia Sharman was the first British citizen to go into space. Sharman received a bachelor's degree in chemistry from the University of Sheffield in 1984. After receiving a doctorate from Birbeck College, London, she worked first as an engineer in London and then as a chemist for Mars Confectionery Ltd.

In November 1989 she responded to a radio advertisement for astronauts and was selected from more than 13,000 applicants to be part of Project Juno, a commercial British cosmonaut mission. She underwent 18 months of rigorous training at the Yury Gagarin Cosmonaut Training Centre at Star City, Russia. The project was nearly called off because the Juno consortium could not raise the required funding. The mission was able to proceed with Soviet money; however, the British experiments were limited owing to budgetary concerns.

Sharman finally launched into space on May 18, 1991, as a research cosmonaut on board Soyuz TM-12 with two Soviet cosmonauts, commander Anatoly Artsebarsky and flight engineer Sergey Krikalyov. Soyuz TM-12 docked with the space station Mir on May 20. The mission lasted nearly eight days, during which time Sharman conducted medical and agricultural tests. She also communicated with British schoolchildren on the radio. Sharman returned to Earth aboard Soyuz TM-11 on May 26.

Sharman was on the short list of candidates when the European Space Agency selected astronauts in 1992 and 1998. However, she was not selected in the final astronaut groups. She was made an Officer of the Order of the British Empire in 1992.

SHEIKH MUSZAPHAR SHUKOR
(b. July 27, 1972, Kuala Lumpur, Malay.)

Orthopedic surgeon Sheikh Muszaphar Shukor was the first Malaysian to go into space. Sheikh earned a degree in medicine and surgery at Kasturba Medical College in Manipal, India. He also earned an advanced degree in orthopedic surgery at University Kebangsaan, Kuala Lumpur, Malay., and became an orthopedist at University Kebangsaan Malaysia Hospital.

Sheikh was selected in 2006 from among 11,000 applicants to enter the Malaysian spaceflight program, Angkasawan. Angkasawan was the product of a Malaysian-Russian agreement in which Malaysia purchased 18 Russian fighter jets and Russia arranged to train and fly a Malaysian cosmonaut on a mission to the International Space Station.

Sheikh became a national celebrity as the Malaysian press followed the preparations for his 10-day journey. On Oct. 10, 2007, Sheikh was launched from the Baikonur Cosmodrome in Kazakhstan to the ISS on Soyuz TMA-11 with commander Yury Malenchenko of Russia and flight engineer Peggy Whitson of the United States. He faced the challenge of becoming the first Muslim to observe Ramadan in space. To assist him with the difficulty of performing daily rites on a ship that orbited Earth 16 times every 24 hours, the Malaysian government assembled 150 clerics and scientists who produced a booklet titled "Guidelines for Performing Islamic Rites at the International Space Station."

While aboard the space station, Sheikh performed industrial and medical scientific experiments and recorded video addresses for schoolchildren. He returned to Earth on board Soyuz TMA-10 on October 21.

MARK SHUTTLEWORTH
(b. Sept. 18, 1973, Welkom, S.Af.)

Entrepreneur, philanthropist, and space tourist, Mark Shuttleworth was the first South African in space. Shuttleworth was a student at the University of Cape Town in 1995 when he founded Thawte, a consulting firm that became a world leader in Internet security for electronic commerce. He sold the firm in 1999 to the U.S.-based company VeriSign and with his profits founded a venture capital firm and a nonprofit organization dedicated to funding education initiatives in Africa.

In 2001, at a personal cost of $20 million, Shuttleworth bought a seat on a Russian spacecraft and began the First African in Space project. For nearly a year he trained in Star City, Russia, and in Kazakhstan for a mission aboard a Soyuz capsule to the International Space Station (ISS). On April 25, 2002, Shuttleworth lifted off on Soyuz TM-34 with two cosmonauts, commander Yury Gidzenko of Russia and flight engineer Roberto Vittori of Italy, from the Baikonur Cosmodrome in Kazakhstan and docked two days later at the ISS. Shuttleworth spent eight days aboard the space station, where he conducted scientific experiments for South Africa. He returned to Earth aboard Soyuz TM-33 on May 5, 2002.

Upon returning, Shuttleworth traveled widely and spoke about spaceflight to schoolchildren around the world. He returned to his work in technology and in 2004 founded Ubuntu, a project that created desktop and operating system software for free distribution to computer users, with a special focus on expanding personal computer access in developing countries.

PHAM TUAN
(b. Feb. 14, 1947, Quôc Tuân, Viet.)

Pilot and cosmonaut Pham Tuan was the first Vietnamese citizen in space. Tuan joined the Vietnam People's Air Force in 1965, where he became a pilot and engineer. During the Vietnam War he flew combat missions against American fighter planes and in 1972 won the praise of his government, which claimed that Tuan had become the first person ever to shoot down an American B-52 bomber, although the United States government claimed that B-52s were brought down only by surface-to-air missiles.

In 1979, four years after the reunification of Vietnam and the withdrawal of American military forces, the Vietnamese government selected Tuan to represent his country in the Soviet Union's Intercosmos program. In the Intercosmos program, non-Soviet cosmonauts flew alongside experienced Soviet crews on routine missions staged to demonstrate solidarity with Warsaw Pact and other countries sympathetic to the Soviet Union.

On July 23, 1980, Tuan lifted off from the Baikonur Cosmodrome in Kazakhstan aboard Soyuz 37 with Soviet cosmonaut Viktor Gorbatko. Tuan flew as a research cosmonaut on a mission that lasted nearly eight days, including six days on the Salyut 6 space station, where he conducted scientific experiments. He and Gorbatko returned aboard Soyuz 36 on July 31.

Upon his return Tuan was named a Hero of the Soviet Union and celebrated as a Vietnamese national hero. He returned to military service, where he became lieutenant general in the air force. He later joined the National Assembly and was named chairman of the General Department for Defense Industry. He retired from the air force in 2008.

FRANZ VIEHBÖCK
(b. Aug. 24, 1960, Perchtoldsdorf, Austria)

Austrian electrical engineer and cosmonaut Franz Artur Viehböck was the first Austrian to go into space. Viehböck graduated from the Vienna University of Technology with a master's degree in electrical and electronic engineering and later earned a doctorate in electronic engineering. He was an assistant professor at the Vienna University of Technology's Institute of Electrical Measurements and Circuit Design.

Viehböck was selected for Austromir-91, a joint Soviet-Austrian space mission, in October 1989. He trained at the Yury Gagarin Cosmonaut Training Centre in Star City, U.S.S.R. (now Russia), for two years. He flew into space on Soyuz TM-13 as a research cosmonaut on Oct. 2, 1991, with two Soviet cosmonauts, commander Aleksandr Volkov and research cosmonaut Toktar Aubakirov. Viehböck and his crewmates were transported to the Mir space station, where they conducted scientific and technical experiments in the fields of materials processing, physics, and space medicine. He returned to Earth aboard Soyuz TM-12, landing on Oct. 10, 1991.

After his spaceflight, Viehböck toured Austria and gave lectures on his space mission. In 1994 he joined the space systems division of the American defense company Rockwell International as a program development manager, working primarily on joint programs with aerospace companies based in Europe and the former Soviet Union. In 1997 he directed the international business development department in the space systems division of the American aerospace corporation Boeing North American. Later that year Viehböck was promoted to director of international programs of Boeing's new space systems unit, and in June 1999 he became Boeing's country director in Austria and the European representative of Boeing's space and communications group.

In March 2000 Viehböck was appointed technology adviser to the governor of Lower Austria. In 2002 Viehböck became the president of Berndorf Band GmbH, an Austrian manufacturer of endless steel belts. In

January 2008 he was made a member of the board of the Berndorf Corporation.

YANG LIWEI
(b. June 21, 1965, Suizhong, Liaoning, China)

Yang Liwei was the first person sent into space by the Chinese space program. In 1983 he enlisted in the Chinese People's Liberation Army (PLA), where he was chosen to enter the aviation college of the PLA Air Force. He graduated in 1987 and became a fighter pilot, accumulating more than 1,350 flight hours. In 1998 he was selected from more than 1,500 candidates to enter astronaut training for China's manned spaceflight program. With 11 other taikonauts (the Chinese equivalent of astronauts), Yang spent five years studying the science and operation of spacecraft and undergoing physical and psychological training.

Yang was identified as the crew member for China's first manned spaceflight only one day before the scheduled launch of the Shenzhou 5 craft. On Oct. 15, 2003, he lifted off from the Jiuquan Satellite Launch Centre in the Gobi desert in China's Gansu province. A Chang Zheng 2F rocket boosted Shenzhou 5 into space, where Yang spent 21 hours and orbited Earth 14 times. He never entered the craft's orbital module, which was released to perform a six-month military imaging reconnaissance mission. On October 16 he returned aboard the reentry module, which parachuted to the ground near a landing site in Inner Mongolia.

Following Yang's return, he was named vice-commander-in-chief of the astronauts system of China's manned spaceflight project. In 2008 Yang was promoted to major general.

YI SOYEON
(b. June 2, 1978, Kwangju, S.Kor.)

Scientist and astronaut Yi Soyeon was the first South Korean citizen in space. She earned bachelor's and master's degrees in mechanical engineering at the Korea Advanced Institute of Science and Technology (KAIST) in Taejon in 2001 and 2002, respectively.

In 2006 she was working toward a doctorate in biological science at KAIST when she was one of two finalists selected from 36,000 applicants to train in Russia for a flight to the International Space Station (ISS). South Korea paid Russia $20 million to allow a South Korean cosmonaut to accompany the Russian spaceflight. Yi was trained as a backup to computer engineer Ko San. The Russian Federal Space Agency, however, barred Ko from the mission for violations of training protocol after he removed reading materials from a training centre and mailed classified documents to South Korea.

On April 8, 2008, Yi blasted off from the Baikonur Cosmodrome in Kazakhstan as a payload specialist alongside two Russian cosmonauts, commander Sergey Volkov and flight engineer Oleg Kononenko. Their Soyuz TMA-12 craft docked with the ISS, where Yi spent nine days carrying out experiments and medical tests. She returned on April 19 with two returning space station crew members, American commander Peggy Whitson and Russian flight engineer Yury Malenchenko, aboard Soyuz TMA-11.

Although the mission was a success, the Soyuz's equipment module failed to separate properly from the reentry module, and so the craft followed an unusually steep trajectory to Earth and made a rough landing in the Kazakhstan steppes, during which Yi sustained back injuries that later required her hospitalization.

ZHAI ZHIGANG
(b. Oct. 10, 1966, Longjiang, Qiqihar, Heilongjiang, China)

Chinese astronaut Zhai Zhigang performed China's first space walk. Zhai was the child of an illiterate mother who peddled sunflower seeds to pay for her children's education. He joined the Chinese People's Liberation Army (PLA) and won entry into the PLA Army Air Force Aviation Institute, where he became a fighter pilot. As a pilot he logged 1,000 hours of flight time and rose to the rank of colonel. He was selected from more than 1,500 candidates in 1998 to enter astronaut training for China's manned spaceflight program.

With a dozen other taikonauts (the Chinese equivalent of astronauts), he spent five years studying the science and operation of spacecraft and undergoing physical and psychological training. In 2003 he was among the final candidates to pilot Shenzhou 5, China's first manned spaceflight, and served as the backup to Chinese astronaut Yang Liwei. He was again a backup in 2006 for the Shenzhou 6 mission.

On Sept. 25, 2008, after 10 years of waiting and preparation, Zhai lifted off as commander with two other crew members, Liu Buoming and Jing Haipeng, aboard Shenzhou 7 from the Jiuquan Satellite Launch Centre in Gansu province, northwestern China. The crew spent three days in Earth orbit. On the second day, as a camera broadcast the event live to audiences in China, Zhai left the orbital module to walk in space. The crew returned safely to Earth on September 27 in the Shenzhou's reentry module, which parachuted to the ground in the northern grasslands of China.

Appendix: Achievements in Space

CHRONOLOGY OF NOTABLE ASTRONAUTS			
NAME	MISSION	DATE	ACCOMPLISHMENT
Yury Gagarin	Vostok 1	April 12, 1961	First man in space
Alan Shepard	Mercury-Redstone 3 (*Freedom 7*)	May 5, 1961	First American in space
Gherman Titov	Vostok 2	Aug. 6, 1961	First to spend more than one day in space; youngest person (25 years old) in space
John Glenn	Mercury-Atlas 6 (*Friendship 7*)	Feb. 20, 1962	First American in orbit
	STS-95 (*Discovery*)	Oct. 28–Nov. 7, 1998	Oldest person (77 years old) in space
Adriyan Nikolayev; Pavel Popovich	Vostok 3; Vostok 4	Aug. 11–15, 1962; Aug. 12–15, 1962	First simultaneous flight of two spacecraft
Valentina Tereshkova	Vostok 6	June 16–19, 1963	First woman in space
Konstantin Feoktistov; Vladimir Komarov; Boris Yegorov	Voshkod 1	Oct. 12–13, 1964	First multimanned spacecraft; first doctor in space (Yegorov)
Aleksey Leonov	Voshkod 2	March 18–19, 1965	First person to walk in space
Roger Chaffee; Virgil Grissom; Edward White II	Apollo 1	Jan. 27, 1967	Killed in fire while testing spacecraft
Vladimir Komarov	Soyuz 1	April 23–24, 1967	First spaceflight casualty
William Anders; Frank Borman; James Lovell	Apollo 8	Dec. 21–27, 1968	First to fly around the Moon

NAME	MISSION	DATE	ACCOMPLISHMENT
Neil Armstrong; Edwin ("Buzz") Aldrin	Apollo 11	July 16–24, 1969	First to walk on the Moon
Fred Haise; James Lovell; Jack Swigert	Apollo 13	April 11–17, 1970	Farthest from Earth (401,056 km [249,205 miles]); survived oxygen-tank explosion
Georgy Dobrovolsky; Viktor Patsayev; Vladislav Volkov	Soyuz 11/Salyut 1	June 6–29, 1971	First stay on a space station; first to die in space
Eugene Cernan; Harrison Schmitt	Apollo 17	Dec. 7–19, 1972	Last to walk on the Moon
Vance Brand; Donald Slayton; Thomas Stafford; Valery Kubasov; Aleksey Leonov	Apollo-Soyuz	July 17–19, 1975	First joint U.S.-Soviet spaceflight
Sigmund Jähn	Soyuz 31/Salyut 6/ Soyuz 29	Aug. 26–Sept. 3, 1978	First German astronaut in space
Jean-Loup Chrétien	Soyuz T-6/Salyut 7	June 24–July 2, 1982	First French astronaut in space
Sally Ride	STS-7 (Challenger)	June 18–24, 1983	First American woman in space
Guion Bluford	STS-8 (Challenger)	Aug. 30–Sept. 5, 1983	First African American in space
Ulf Merbold	STS-9 (Columbia)	Nov. 28–Dec. 8, 1983	First ESA astronaut in space
Rakesh Sharma	Soyuz T-11/Salyut 7	April 3–11, 1984	First Indian in space
Marc Garneau	STS-41-G (Challenger)	Oct. 5–13, 1984	First Canadian in space
Franklin Chang-Díaz	STS-61-C (Columbia)	Jan. 12–18, 1986	First Hispanic American in space

NAME	MISSION	DATE	ACCOMPLISHMENT
Christa McAuliffe	STS-51-L (*Challenger*)	Jan. 28, 1986	Was to have been the first teacher in space; killed in *Challenger* explosion
Akiyama Tohiro	Soyuz TM-11/Mir/ Soyuz TM-10	Dec. 2–10, 1990	First Japanese in space; first commercial astronaut
Helen Sharman	Soyuz TM-12/Mir/ Soyuz TM-11	May 18–26, 1991	First Briton in space; first non-U.S., non-Russian female astronaut
Mae Jemison; Mohri Mamoru	STS-47 (*Endeavour*)	Sept. 12–20, 1992	First African American woman in space; first Japanese astronaut in space
Ellen Ochoa	STS-56 (*Discovery*)	April 8–17, 1993	First Hispanic American woman in space
Valery Polyakov	Soyuz TM-18/Mir/ Soyuz TM-20	Jan. 8, 1994– March 22, 1995	Longest stay in space (438 days)
Sergey Krikalyov	STS-60 (*Discovery*)	Feb. 3–11, 1994	First Russian on U.S. spacecraft
Eileen Collins	STS-93 (*Columbia*)	July 23–28, 1999	First female space shuttle commander
Dennis Tito	Soyuz TM-32/ISS/ Soyuz TM-31	April 28–May 6, 2001	First space tourist
Jerry Ross	STS-110 (*Atlantis*)/ ISS	April 8–19, 2002	First person to fly to space seven times
Yang Liwei	Shenzhou 5	Oct. 15, 2003	First Chinese astronaut in space
Michael Melvill	SpaceShipOne	June 21, 2004	First private spaceflight
Yi Soyeon	Soyuz TMA-12/ISS/ Soyuz TMA-11	April 8–19, 2008	First Korean astronaut in space

SPACE STATIONS FROM 1971					
STATION, OR MAJOR MODULE FOR MODULAR STATION	COUNTRY OF ORIGIN, OR COUNTRY OF LAUNCH FOR ISS* MODULES	DATE LAUNCHED	DATE REENTERED	OCCUPANCY, TOTAL DAYS (AND NUMBER OF MAJOR EXPEDITIONS)	COMMENTS
Salyut 1	U.S.S.R.	April 19, 1971	Oct. 11, 1971	23 (1)	First space station, equipped for scientific studies; abandoned after its first crew died returning to Earth
Salyut 2	U.S.S.R.	April 3, 1973	May 28, 1973	0	Military reconnaissance platform; suffered explosion after achieving orbit and was never occupied
Cosmos 557	U.S.S.R.	May 11, 1973	May 22, 1973	0	Scientific station; crippled after achieving orbit and was never occupied
Skylab	U.S.	May 14, 1973	July 11, 1979	171 (3)	First U.S. space station; successfully supported solar studies and biomedical experiments on the effects of weightlessness
Salyut 3	U.S.S.R.	June 25, 1974	Jan. 24, 1975	16 (1)	Military reconnaissance platform
Salyut 4	U.S.S.R.	Dec. 26, 1974	Feb. 3, 1977	93 (2)	Scientific station; operated until its systems were exhausted
Salyut 5	U.S.S.R.	June 22, 1976	Aug. 8, 1977	67 (2)	Military reconnaissance platform

Station, or Major Module for Modular Station	Country of Origin, or Country of Launch for ISS* Modules	Date Launched	Date Reentered	Occupancy, Total Days (and Number of Major Expeditions)	Comments
Salyut 6	U.S.S.R.	Sept. 29, 1977	July 29, 1982	684 (6)	First second-generation Salyut, operated as highly successful scientific station; resident crews hosted a series of international visitors
Salyut 7	U.S.S.R.	April 19, 1982	Feb. 2, 1991	815 (5)	Problem-plagued follow-on to Salyut 6 that had to be repeatedly rescued
Mir (modular)	U.S.S.R./ Russia	March 23, 2001	Occupied March 14, 1986, to June 15, 2000 (continuously from Sept. 7, 1989, to Aug. 28, 1999)		First space station assembled in orbit using individually launched, specialized modules; successfully applied lessons learned from Salyut program
Mir base block		Feb. 20, 1986			Habitat module
Kvant 1		March 31, 1987			Astrophysics observatory with X-ray telescopes
Kvant 2		Nov. 26, 1989			Supplementary life-support systems and large air lock

Station, or Major Module for Modular Station	Country of Origin, or Country of Launch for ISS* Modules	Date Launched	Date Reentered	Occupancy, Total Days (And Number of Major Expeditions)	Comments
Kristall		May 31, 1990			Microgravity materials-processing laboratory
Spektr		May 20, 1995			Module with apparatus for NASA research
Priroda		April 23, 1996			Module with NASA apparatus and Earth-sciences sensors
International Space Station (modular)	International consortium, primarily U.S. and Russia			Permanently occupied since Nov. 2, 2000	Modular expandable station intended to serve world's space agencies for first quarter of 21st century
Zarya	Russia	Nov. 20, 1998			U.S.-funded, Russian-built module supplying initial solar power and attitude-control system
Unity	U.S.	Dec. 4, 1998			U.S.-built connecting node
Zvezda	Russia	July 2, 2000			Russian-built habitat module and control centre
Destiny	U.S.	Feb. 7, 2001			U.S.-built NASA microgravity laboratory

Station, or Major Module for Modular Station	Country of Origin, or Country of Launch for ISS* Modules	Date Launched	Date Reentered	Occupancy, Total Days (And Number of Major Expeditions)	Comments
Quest	U.S.	July 12, 2001			U.S.-built air lock allowing station-based space walks for U.S. and Russian astronauts
Pirs	Russia	Sept. 14, 2001			Russian-built docking compartment providing Soyuz docking port and additional air lock for Russian space walks
Harmony	U.S.	Oct. 23, 2007			U.S.-built connecting node
Columbus	U.S.	Feb. 7, 2008			European Space Agency-built micro-gravity laboratory
Kibo	U.S.	March 11, 2008; May 31, 2008			Japanese-built micro-gravity laboratory
Dextre	U.S.	March 11, 2008			Canadian-built robot

*International Space Station

ENDURANCE RECORDS			
COSMONAUT/ ASTRONAUT	PRIMARY HABITAT	MONTH AND YEAR LAUNCHED	DAYS IN SPACE
Yury A. Gagarin	Vostok 1	April 1961	0.07
Gherman S. Titov	Vostok 2	August 1961	1.05
Andriyan G. Nikolayev	Vostok 3	August 1962	3.93
Valery F. Bykovsky	Vostok 5	June 1963	4.97
L. Gordon Cooper, Jr.; Charles Conrad, Jr.	Gemini 5	August 1965	7.92
Frank Borman; James A. Lovell, Jr.	Gemini 7	December 1965	13.75
Andriyan G. Nikolayev; Vitaly I. Sevastyanov	Soyuz 9	June 1970	17.71
Georgy T. Dobrovolsky; Viktor I. Patsayev; Vladislav N. Volkov	Salyut 1	June 1971	23.76
Charles Conrad, Jr.; Paul J. Weitz; Joseph P. Kerwin	Skylab	May 1973	28.04
Alan L. Bean; Jack R. Lousma; Owen K. Garriott	Skylab	July 1973	59.49
Gerald P. Carr; William R. Pogue; Edward G. Gibson	Skylab	November 1973	84.04
Yury V. Romanenko; Georgy M. Grechko	Salyut 6	December 1977	96.42
Vladimir V. Kovalyonok; Aleksandr S. Ivanchenkov	Salyut 6	June 1978	139.6
Vladimir A. Lyakhov; Valery V. Ryumin	Salyut 6	February 1979	175.06
Leonid I. Popov; Valery V. Ryumin	Salyut 6	April 1980	184.84
Anatoly N. Berezovoy; Valentin V. Lebedev	Salyut 7	May 1982	211.38

Cosmonaut/ Astronaut	Primary Habitat	Month and Year Launched	Days in Space
Leonid D. Kizim; Vladimir A. Solovyov; Oleg Y. Atkov	Salyut 7	February 1984	236.95
Yury V. Romanenko	Mir	February 1987	326.48
Vladimir G. Titov; Musa K. Manarov	Mir	December 1987	365.95
Valery V. Polyakov	Mir	January 1994	437.75

SIGNIFICANT MILESTONES IN SPACE EXPLORATION			
DATE ACCOMPLISHED	EVENT	DETAILS	COUNTRY OR AGENCY
Oct. 4, 1957	First artificial Earth satellite	Sputnik 1	U.S.S.R.
Nov. 3, 1957	First animal launched into space	Dog Laika aboard Sputnik 2	U.S.S.R.
Sept. 14, 1959	First spacecraft to hard-land on another celestial object (the Moon)	Luna 2	U.S.S.R.
Oct. 7, 1959	First pictures of the far side of the Moon	Luna 3	U.S.S.R.
April 1, 1960	First applications satellite launched	TIROS 1 (weather observation)	U.S.
Aug. 11, 1960	First recovery of a payload from Earth orbit	Discoverer 13 (part of Corona recon-naissance satellite program)	U.S.
April 12, 1961	First human to orbit Earth	Yury Gagarin on Vostok 1	U.S.S.R.
Dec. 14, 1962	First data returned from another planet (Venus)	Mariner 2	U.S.
June 16, 1963	First woman in space	Valentina Tereshkova on Vostok 6	U.S.S.R.
July 26, 1963	First satellite to operate in geo-stationary orbit	Syncom 2 (telecom-munications satellite)	U.S.
March 18, 1965	First space walk	Aleksey Leonov on Voskhod 2	U.S.S.R.
July 14, 1965	First spacecraft pictures of Mars	Mariner 4	U.S.

Date Accomplished	Event	Details	Country or Agency
Feb. 3, 1966	First spacecraft to soft-land on the Moon	Luna 9	U.S.S.R.
April 24, 1967	First death during a space mission	Vladimir Komarov on Soyuz 1	U.S.S.R.
Dec. 24, 1968	First humans to orbit the Moon	Frank Borman, James Lovell, and William Anders on Apollo 8	U.S.
July 20, 1969	First human to walk on the Moon	Neil Armstrong on Apollo 11	U.S.
Sept. 24, 1970	First return of lunar samples by an unmanned spacecraft	Luna 16	U.S.S.R.
Dec. 15, 1970	First soft landing on another planet (Venus)	Venera 7	U.S.S.R.
April 19, 1971	First space station launched	Salyut 1	U.S.S.R.
Nov. 13, 1971	First spacecraft to orbit another planet (Mars)	Mariner 9	U.S.
Dec. 2, 1971	First spacecraft to soft-land on Mars	Mars 3	U.S.S.R.
Dec. 3, 1973	First spacecraft to fly by Jupiter	Pioneer 10	U.S.
July 17, 1975	First international docking in space	Apollo and Soyuz spacecraft during Apollo-Soyuz Test Project	U.S., U.S.S.R.

Date Accomplished	Event	Details	Country or Agency
July 20, 1976	First pictures transmitted from the surface of Mars	Viking 1	U.S.
Sept. 1, 1979	First spacecraft to fly by Saturn	Pioneer 11	U.S.
April 12-14, 1981	First reusable spacecraft launched and returned from space	Space shuttle Columbia	U.S.
Jan. 24, 1986	First spacecraft to fly by Uranus	Voyager 2	U.S.
March 13, 1986	First spacecraft to make a close flyby of a comet nucleus	Giotto at Halley's Comet	European Space Agency
Aug. 24, 1989	First spacecraft to fly by Neptune	Voyager 2	U.S.
April 25, 1990	First large optical space telescope launched	Hubble Space Telescope	U.S., European Space Agency
Dec. 7, 1995	First spacecraft to orbit Jupiter	*Galileo*	U.S.
Nov. 2, 2000	First resident crew to occupy the International Space Station	William Shepherd, Yury Gidzenko, and Sergey Krikalyov	U.S., Russia
Feb. 12, 2001	First spacecraft to orbit (2000) and land on (2001) an asteroid	NEAR at the asteroid Eros	U.S.
June 21, 2004	First privately funded manned spacecraft to achieve suborbital flight above 100 km (62 miles)	SpaceShipOne	Mojave Aerospace Ventures (commercial joint venture)

Date Accomplished	Event	Details	Country or Agency
July 1, 2004	First spacecraft to orbit Saturn	Cassini-Huygens	U.S., European Space Agency, Italy
Jan. 14, 2005	First spacecraft to land on the moon of a planet other than Earth (Saturn's moon Titan)	Huygens probe of the Cassini-Huygens spacecraft	U.S., European Space Agency, Italy

GLOSSARY

aerodynamics The science that deals with the motion of air and other gaseous fluids, and forces acting on bodies in motion relative to the air and such fluids.

aeronautics Having to do with aircraft design, construction, and navigation.

ballistic Relates to projectiles, such as rockets or missiles, moving with their own initial momentum under the force of gravity.

booster rocket Rocket that lifts a spacecraft to orbit; also called a step rocket.

circumlunar Revolving or traveling around the Moon.

combustion A chemical change, involving heat and light, capable of propelling a vehicle.

extravehicular activity (EVA) Activity that takes place outside of spacecraft or a space station, such as a space walk.

International Geophysical Year (IGY) A worldwide program of geophysical research that was conducted from July 1957 to December 1958. The first satellites were launched as part of IGY.

interplanetary Existing or occurring between planets.

launch vehicle A rocket-powered vehicle that lifts spacecraft into orbit.

lunar Anything that involves, affects, or is affected by the Moon.

microgravity Feeling very little gravitational force; another term for the feeling of weightlessness in space.

mission specialist A person trained to have a specific primary responsibility during a spaceflight mission.

module A self-contained unit within spacecraft that is used for a specific environment or purpose.

orbital Following the path a heavenly body takes in its periodical revolution around another body in outer space.

O-ring A rubber or plastic gasket that acts as a seal, protecting against excess pressure; a faulty O-ring is blamed for the *Challenger* shuttle disaster.

overflights When satellites or other spacecraft travel freely over any point on Earth while in orbit, without consideration of earthly territorial boundaries.

payload The crew, equipment, instruments, and possible passengers (space tourists) carried by spacecraft into orbit.

propellant Fuel capable of providing thrust, which lifts a vehicle into the air or into space.

radiometric age dating Determining the age of rock by measuring the decay level of radioactive isotopes found within its structure.

reconnaissance Exploring or inspecting a geographic area for the purpose of collecting data.

rocketry The technology behind rocket design, construction, and flight.

satellite An object that orbits a planet or other celestial body; there are natural satellites (moons) and artificial satellites, which are launched into orbit.

solar array An arrangement of cells that collect energy from the Sun.

space sickness An illness caused by an imbalance to the inner ear because of weightlessness; symptoms include nausea and vomiting.

space truck How NASA originally referred to the space shuttle, because it "trucked" cargo and people to interstellar locations.

splashdown The landing of a spacecraft or missile in water; early spacecraft, before shuttles, traditionally splashed down in an ocean after a mission was over.

suborbital Having or following a trajectory of less than one orbit.

taikonaut A Chinese astronaut.

tectonic Relating to changes to the structure of a planetary or other celestial body's surface.

theoretical Based on theory, not practical application.

thrust To push, or drive, with force.

trajectory The course or path taken by spacecraft and projectiles such as missiles.

vacuum Space that is devoid of matter.

velocity The speed at which an action occurs.

For Further Reading

Ashford, David. *Spaceflight Revolution.* London, England: Imperial College Press (dist. by World Scientific Publishing Co. Pte. Ltd.), 2002.

Boomhower, Ray E. *Gus Grissom: The Lost Astronaut.* Indianapolis, IN: Indiana Historical Society Press, 2004.

Burleson, Daphne. *Space Programs Outside the United States: All Exploration and Research Efforts, Country by Country.* Jefferson, NC: McFarland & Company, Inc., 2005.

Burgess, Colin, etal. *Fallen Astronauts: Heroes Who Died Reaching for the Moon.* Lincoln, NE: University of Nebraska Press, 2003.

Catchpole, John E. *The International Space Station: Building for the Future.* Chichester, England: Praxis Publishing, Ltd., 2008.

Chaikin, Andrew. *Voices from the Moon: Apollo Astronauts Describe Their Lunar Experiences.* New York, NY: Viking Studio, 2009.

Collins, Michael. *Carrying the Fire: An Astronaut's Journeys* (Fortieth Anniversary Edition). New York, NY: Farrar, Strauss and Giroux, 2009.

Cook, Richard C. Challenger *Revealed: An Insider's Account of How the Reagan Administration Caused the Greatest Tragedy of the Space Age.* New York, NY: Avalon Publishing Group, 2006.

Cooper, Gordon. *Leap of Faith: An Astronaut's Journey into the Unknown.* New York, NY: HarperCollins, 2000.

D'Antonio, Michael. *A Ball, a Dog, and a Monkey: 1957—The Space Race Begins.* New York, NY: Simon and Schuster, 2007.

Darling, David. *The Complete Book of Spaceflight: From Apollo 1 to Zero Gravity.* Hoboken, NJ: John Wiley & Sons, Inc., 2003.

Dreer, Francis. *Space Conquest: The Complete History of Manned Spaceflight.* Somerset, England: Haynes Publishing, 2009.

Duggins, Pat. *Final Countdown: NASA and the End of the Space Shuttle Program.* Gainesville, FL: University Press of Florida, 2009.

French, Francis, and Carl Burgess. *In the Shadow of the Moon: A Challenging Journey to Tranquility, 1965-1969.* Lincoln, NE: University of Nebraska Press, 2007.

French, Francis, and Carl Burgess. *Into That Silent Sea: Trailblazers of the Space Era, 1961-1965.* Lincoln, NE: University of Nebraska Press, 2007.

Furniss, Tim, David J. Shayler, and Michael D. Praxis. *Manned Spaceflight Log: 1961-2006.* Birmingham, England: Spring-Praxis Books, 2007.

Glenn, John. *John Glenn: A Memoir.* New York, NY: Bantam, 2000.

Harland, David M. *The Story of Space Station Mir*. New York, NY: Springer-Verlag, 2005.

Hickam, Homer H., Jr. *Rocket Boys*. New York, NY: Delta, 2000.

Jones, Tom. *Sky Walking: An Astronaut's Memoir*. New York, NY; HarperCollins, 2007.

Linenger, Jerry. *Letters from MIR: An Astronaut's Letters to His Son*. Columbus, OH: McGraw-Hill, 2003.

Mindell, David. *Digital Apollo: Human and Machine in Spaceflight*. Boston, MA: MIT Press, 2008.

Mullane, Mike. *Riding Rockets: The Outrageous Tales of a Space Shuttle Astronaut*. New York, NY: Scribner, 2006.

Neufeld, Michael J. *Von Braun: Dreamer of Space, Engineer of War*. New York, NY: Vintage/Anchor Books, 2008.

Oberg, James. *Star-Crossed Orbits: Inside the U.S.-Russian Space Alliance*. Columbus, OH: McGraw-Hill, 2002.

Phillips Mackowski, Maura. *Testing the Limits: Aviation Medicine and the Origins of Manned Spaceflight*. College Station, TX: Texas A&M University Press, 2006.

Reeves-Stevens, Garfield, and Judith Reeves-Stevens. *Going to Mars: The Stories of People Behind NASA's Mars Missions Past, Present, and Future*. New York, NY: Simon and Schuster, Inc., 2004.

Rogers, Lucy. *It's ONLY Rocket Science: An Introduction in Plain English*. New York, NY: Springer Science + Business Media, LLC, 2008.

Rycroft, M.J (ed.). *Beyond the International Space Station: The Future of Human Spaceflight*. AA Dordrecht, the Netherlands: Kluwer Academic Publishers, 2002.

Sacknoff, Scott (ed.). *In Their Own Words: Conversations With the Astronauts and Men Who Led America's Journey into Space and to the Moon*. Casper, WY: Space Publications LLC, 2003.

Seedhouse, Erik. *Tourists in Space: A Practical Guide*. Chichester, England: Praxis Publishing, Ltd., 2008.

Shayler, David J. *Disasters and Accidents in Manned Spaceflight*. Birmingham, England: Springer-Praxis Books, 2009.

Sparrow, Giles. *Spaceflight: The Complete Story from Sputnik to Shuttle*. New York, NY: DK Adult, 2007.

Swinerd, Graham. *How Spacecraft Fly: Spaceflight Without Formulae*. Hampshire, England; Springer, 2008.

Wylie, D.M. *Three Decades to a Space Shuttle*. Bloomington, IN: Trafford Publishing, 2006.

INDEX

11/10